To Fellow Dads Everywhere...

You hold in your hands a book that comes from our hearts.

We're fathers. We take the responsibility seriously, and frankly, no task on this earth has challenged us more.

If you're like us, you love your kids with all your heart. You want to be a good dad. You might be part of a nuclear family or among the growing number of divorced or blended families. In any case God has entrusted one or more precious lives into your care and you want to build strong kids who will go on to be responsible, caring adults.

We dads have the privilege, and the responsibility, to help make a significant difference in the next generation of our world — by how we express love and relate to our children!

We want you to be challenged, encouraged and motivated to action by the ideas in *The Dad Difference.* And we invite you to make the commitment with us that, no matter how tough it may get, no matter how unresponsive our kids may be, no matter which way the road may bend in the future — we dedicate ourselves to the privilege and responsibility of conscientious, loving, involved, communicative fathering.

In this book, we'll share some good tips to help you carry through.

Josh McDowell
Norm Wakefield

The Dad Difference

CREATING AN ENVIRONMENT FOR
YOUR CHILD'S SEXUAL WHOLENESS

JOSH McDOWELL
DR. NORM WAKEFIELD

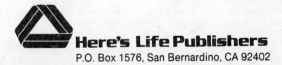

Here's Life Publishers

P.O. Box 1576, San Bernardino, CA 92402

First printing, July 1989
Second printing, October 1989

Published by
HERE'S LIFE PUBLISHERS, INC.
P. O. Box 1576
San Bernardino, CA 92402

Library of Congress Cataloging-in-Publication Data
McDowell, Josh.
    The dad difference : creating an environment for your child's sexual
wholeness / Josh McDowell and Norm Wakefield.
    p.   cm.
    ISBN 0-89840-252-2
    1. Fathers—Religious life.   2. Parenting—Religious aspects—Chris-
tianity.   3. Sex role—Religious aspects—Christianity.   I. Wakefield,
Norm.   II. Title.
    BV4846.M37   1989
    248.8'421—dc 19   89-30707
                             CIP

    Unless otherwise indicated, Scripture quotations are from *The Holy
Bible: New International Version,* © 1973, 1978, 1984 by the International
Bible Society. Published by Zondervan Bible Publishers, Grand Rapids,
Michigan.
    Scripture quotations designated NASB are from *The New American
Standard Bible,* © The Lockman Foundation 1960, 1962, 1963, 1968, 1971,
1972, 1975, 1977.
    Scripture quotations designated TLB are from *The Living Bible,* © 1971
by Tyndale House Publishers, Wheaton, Illinois.

For More Information, Write:
L.I.F.E.—P.O. Box A399, Sydney South 2000, Australia
Campus Crusade for Christ of Canada—Box 300, Vancouver, B.C., V6C 2X3, Canada
Campus Crusade for Christ—Pearl Assurance House, 4 Temple Row, Birmingham, B2 5HG, England
Lay Institute for Evangelism—P.O. Box 8786, Auckland 3, New Zealand
Campus Crusade for Christ—P.O. Box 240, Colombo Court Post Office, Singapore 9117
Great Commission Movement of Nigeria—P.O. Box 500, Jos, Plateau State Nigeria, West Africa
Campus Crusade for Christ International—Arrowhead Springs, San Bernardino, CA 92414, U.S.A.

Contents

Acknowledgments

We gladly acknowledge that this book is the result of many people's energy. Our lives have been shaped by parents, friends, teachers and co-workers, and they are genuine contributors to this writing project.

Seven people have encouraged the two of us with their enthusiasm, energy and support. Our wives have been dedicated partners with us in the parenting process. They have made us better dads. Dave and Becky Bellis spent time with us laying the groundwork, brainstorming the outline and reading the manuscript. Les Stobbe, Dan Benson and Barb Sherrill of Here's Life Publishers have been encouraging friends and skilled editors, who went beyond the call of duty in readying this manuscript.

With sincere thanks to the above, we dedicate this book to our kids, whom we love and cherish:

Kelly
Sean
Katie
Heather
(Josh's kids)

Amy
Joel
Jill
Jody
Annette
(Norm's kids)

A Special Note to Moms

We have a sneaking suspicion that many moms will be reading this book—that's great! We know you'll gain valuable insights on effective fathering, but it can't stop there. We encourage you to take the initiative: Make sure *Dad* reads this book.

Up front we want you to know that we are in no way downplaying your important role in your children's lives by addressing this book to dads. We firmly believe in a team approach to parenting: Mom and Dad working together to raise their family. Unfortunately, we see too many dads reneging their responsibilities as parents. Too many men fail to take an active part in their children's lives, leaving the bulk of parenting to Mom.

So we've written this book to help Dad understand his God-designed role and become a true teammate with you in loving, instructing, guiding, cherishing and affirming your kids.

If you're a single mom, you may be concerned about how your kids are affected by not having a father around (whether physically, emotionally or both). If possible, share this book with your children's father. Keeping your kids' welfare in mind, help your ex to be the best possible dad he can be. It's in everyone's best interest, and your kids will love you for it.

If the children's father is no longer around or not a suitable dad, look for mature, godly men in your church who can provide a positive model of Christian manhood for your kids. Perhaps another dad would be willing to include your kids in family outings, or make special efforts to befriend and talk with your kids. You'll see from reading this book what a tremendous influence the father figure has in a child's life. In families where the father figure is absent, it's wise to try to fill this void with a friend who can serve as a positive male role model to your kids.

And for all moms: You, more than anyone else, will determine how your children see their father. You have enormous power either to support Dad in his ministry to his children or to undermine him and make him look incompetent in their eyes. Considering the long-term effects our fathers have on us, we hope you'll choose to build Dad up. We challenge you to be encouraging to your husband in his attempts at fathering, supportive in your words with him and your children, and lovingly confrontive should his actions (or lack of action) warrant it.

Mom, you're important! We'll be praying for you in your efforts to help Dad become all God created him to be.

Discovering
the
Dad Difference
(Josh)

You hold in your hands a book that comes from our hearts.

We're fathers. We take the responsibility seriously, and frankly, no task on this earth has challenged us more.

We've felt the same exhilaration and frustration of fathering that you have felt.

We have both gazed with proud delight at those wiggling newborn bundles in our wives' arms, filled with love and awe at the miracle we had just witnessed.

We have watched those bundles grow into little people. We've seen them crawl, stand up, walk, fall down, stand up, walk, fall down and stand up again as they determined to discover their little worlds.

We have laughed, cried and prayed over them as they grew into adolescence. We have felt the joy of the tender moments and the despair of the not-so-tender times. We have popped the buttons off our shirts with pride, and at times we have wanted to hide.

We've tried our very best to be good dads; sometimes we've excelled and other times we've blown it. And we know the journey is not over.

If you're like us, you love your kids with all your heart. You want to be a good dad. You might be part of a nuclear family or among the growing number of divorced or blended families. In any case God has entrusted one or more precious lives into your care and you want to build strong kids who will go on to be responsible, caring adults.

But if you're like us, you're also like thousands of other dads whose careers require extensive time away from home and drain our energies or preoccupy our thoughts when we are home.

Defaulting Dads: Absent or Uninvolved

Over the past several years, both Norm and I have observed and counseled scores of fellow strugglers — well-meaning dads who feel almost overwhelmed by the job. Many admit that they're fumbling in the juggling act of marriage, career and fatherhood. Most feel trapped by their intense work schedules and the accompanying pressures; by a lack of practical fathering skills; by a lack of good teamwork with their wives or by unhealthy patterns in their own personalities.

And because of these frustrations, too many men have virtually defaulted as fathers, becoming either absentee or uninvolved in their children's day-by-day development. It's a modern-day family tragedy. Consider:

- Dr. Loren Moshen, of the National Institute of Mental Health, analyzed U.S. census figures and found the absence of a father to be a stronger factor than poverty in contributing to juvenile delinquency.

- A group of Yale behavioral scientists studied delinquency in forty-eight cultures around the world and found that crime rates were highest among children-adults who had been raised solely by women.

- Dr. Martin Deutsch found that the father's presence and conversation—especially at dinner time—stimulates a child to perform better at school.[1]
- A study of 1,337 medical doctors who graduated from Johns Hopkins University between 1948 and 1964 found that lack of closeness with parents was the common factor in hypertension, coronary heart disease, malignant tumors, mental illness and suicide.
- A study of thirty-nine teenage girls who were suffering from the anorexia nervosa eating disorder showed that thirty-six of them had one common denominator: the lack of a close relationship with their fathers.
- Johns Hopkins University researchers found that "young, white teenage girls living in fatherless families . . . were 60 percent more likely to have premarital intercourse than those living in two-parent homes."[2]
- Dr. Armand Nicholi's research found that an emotionally or physically absent father contributes to a child's (1) low motivation for achievement; (2) inability to defer immediate gratification for later rewards; (3) low self-esteem; and (4) susceptibility to group influence and to juvenile delinquency.[3]

From our interaction with hundreds of moms, dads and kids, we would agree with these findings. The relationship a child has with his father can make all the difference in the child's self-esteem, regard for others, and sense of purpose.

Christian Teens: A Revealing Study

In 1987 the Josh McDowell Ministry commissioned an in-depth study of evangelical Christian teenagers, utilizing the services of the Barna Research Group. Our goal was two-fold: to discover the sexual attitudes and activities of today's churched youth, and to discover the major factors influencing those teens' sexual attitudes and behavior.

Eight evangelical denominations participated in the study, with a margin for error of plus or minus 3 percent. Of the teenagers surveyed, 82 percent stated that they knew Jesus Christ as their personal Savior, and 79 percent stated that they were actively involved in their church youth program.

The results of the survey revealed some fascinating information about our teens. Among the findings:

- By age 18, 43 percent of these churched youth had experienced sexual intercourse.
- By age 18, 65 percent had engaged in fondling breasts or genitals and/or sexual intercourse.
- 36 percent were unable to state that sexual intercourse before marriage was morally unacceptable.
- 55 percent were unable to state that fondling of breasts or genitals before marriage was morally unacceptable.
- 38 percent cited "friends" as their primary source of information about sex and sexual relations. Twenty-six percent stated that their primary source of such information was "movies," while 23 percent named "parents" and 22 percent listed "television" as their primary information source.

The Dad Difference

The importance of a good relationship with the

father was underscored over and over again. We found that the average teen in an evangelical church spends less than <u>two minutes per day</u> in meaningful conversation with his <u>father,</u> and spends only slightly more than <u>four minutes per day</u> conversing meaningfully with his <u>mother.</u> Yet one in every four young people surveyed stated that they have *never* had a meaningful conversation with their father.

- Sexual contact and promiscuity was much less likely among teenagers who had close relationships with their fathers.

- <u>Only 16 percent did special things with their fathers on a regular basis.</u>

- Teens who perceived that their parents spend a lot of time with them were less likely to have had sexual contact. Among those who said their parents frequently commit time to them, 39 percent had experienced sexual contact, compared to 61 percent who said their parents seldom or never spent time with them.

In seeking data on how teens form their self-image, we found that the five most important variables are:

1. A close relationship with the father.

2. Spending a lot of time with the father.

3. Spending a lot of time with the mother.

4. Feeling secure and loved at home.

5. A grade average of *A* or *B*.

The element that stood out is that <u>our young people seem to place an even greater premium on their relationships with their fathers than with their mothers.</u>

This does not mean that they minimize the significance of their mothers' contribution to their personhood. <u>In most cases, it seems, the mother is there, doing her job, and as a result the youth have come to *expect* her to be accessible, loving, communicative and accepting. With dad, however, the law of supply and demand comes into play.</u> In many cases he is less accessible, involved or communicative. With attention and time from him in short supply, an aura of greater significance is built around that relationship. Just like all of us, our kids crave what they do not have, and in too many cases they do not have a close relationship with their dads.

The bottom line? Dads are of vital importance to their children! Your relationship with your sons and daughters now is a verified factor in their self-esteem, which in turn affects their growth in wisdom, stature, and favor with God and man.

Fellow Strugglers

We write to you not as experts, for when it comes to raising children there really is no such thing. Rather, we are devoted fellow strugglers with you who have learned a few things we want to share. <u>If we dads talk together, pray for each other and encourage each other, we might better face</u> the challenge of guiding our kids through the minefields of modern adolescence toward happy, responsible adulthood.

I write to you as a father of four children, whose ages are 15, 13, 9 and 3 as *The Dad Difference* rolls off the presses. My practical experience to this point has been mostly that of a dad seeking to establish positive relationships with his kids early in their lives, then nurturing those relationships as my kids begin to grow to adulthood. The insight I share in this book will be from that perspective, as well as from what I have learned while counseling with thousands of older teens and young adults who have shared their stories with me almost every day during the nationwide "WHY WAIT?"

campaign the past three years.

My colleague Norm Wakefield is a professional counselor who deals with heartbreaking parent-child stories every day. On the home front, he is more veteran than I. The father of five children, ages 25, 24, 23, 19 and 17 at publication, he has survived the awkward "tweenage" years of all five and at this date is successfully through the teenage years of three of the five. By observing Norm's relationship with his adult kids, it's obvious to me that he and his wife Winnie have done things right, just as my wife Dottie and I are striving to do.

Just two months before the release of this book, Norm stood as best man at the wedding of his twenty-four-year-old son Joel. Norm reflects on the experience:

"Joel's wedding was a special event for me because he had asked his own dad to be his best man. As I stood beside this young man my mind flashed back many years. I remembered when Joel was a tiny preschooler and I was working on a doctoral program in Louisville, Kentucky. I arrived home one day to discover that my son had injured his head in a freak accident. Though he had the strength to stand, he had no sense of balance and his speech was slurred.

"I rushed Joel to the emergency room at the hospital. As the medical team began to do their evaluation I was left alone with my fear and helplessness. The thought that my son might have sustained some permanent brain or nerve damage scared me. All my tender, loving father-feelings welled up and I began to sob as I realized how precious my son was to me and how I valued him. I cried out to the Lord, 'Take good care of my son!'

"Eventually the doctor came with the assuring news that no serious damage had been done. Within twenty-four hours the symptoms disappeared and Joel was quickly back to his energetic self. But I discovered that day how much my son meant to me.

"Then I recalled a time shortly before Joel became a teenager. He had developed a nasty habit of sarcasm toward his sisters. Winnie and I prayed for him, taught positive responses, disciplined him, had him memorize appropriate Scriptures, but nothing seemed to work. I remembered thinking, *Is this child going to grow up to be a pro at putting down women?* The thought was discouraging, and nothing we did seemed to make a dent in his behavior.

"Some months later I happened to take part in a small sharing group with Joel on New Year's Eve. We were asked to share one thing we would like to ask the Lord to change in us during the coming year. Joel replied, 'I'd like God to change the way I talk to my sisters.' Those words were precious to me. I knew that he was not a thoughtless, irresponsible kid. Like all of us, he was simply caught in a sinful pattern that God's power and grace could change. In the months that followed I saw that change begin to take place.

"Now, as I stood beside this twenty-four-year-old son whom I love and respect, I was filled to overflowing with joy. I knew that he, like his sisters, was committed to honor and serve Jesus Christ. I had watched him serve others with a tender heart. He held a genuine love and respect for his sisters and others. And I knew that he was committed to being a loving husband to Lisa, his bride.

"I was genuinely grateful to God for His faithfulness. He had honored Winnie's and my commitment to love, enjoy and nurture our children. In the process, they had become our dearest friends."

What strikes me as I read Norm's story is that a young groom always asks his best friend to be best man at his wedding. Of all Joel's friends, he chose his father.

I'm sure all of us hope and pray for that type of

friendship with our kids when they reach adulthood. We long for the second half of the biblical promise, "Train up a child in the way he should go *and when he is old he will not depart from it.*" But too many of us let the first part slip: *"Train up a child in the way he should go."* That's what *The Dad Difference* is all about — what we should be doing *now* to help assure that the second part of the promise becomes reality.

We dads have the privilege, and the responsibility, to help make the significant difference in the next generation of our world — by how we express love and relate to our children!

We want you to be challenged, encouraged, and motivated to action by the ideas in *The Dad Difference*. At the same time, we understand that some readers may find this book a bit uncomfortable as they realize that they have not been as effective as they could be.

We don't want you to fall into the guilt-trip trap. We know the pressures that today's dad faces. So here are some important suggestions to help you benefit from our time together.

First, *approach fathering from a positive, optimistic perspective.* Look at fathering as a positive, loving influence that will not only enrich your child's life, but also be a means God will use to "stretch" you mentally, emotionally and spiritually. Consider it an important opportunity to invest your life in someone, believing that the time invested will bear fruit for years — perhaps generations — to come.

Second, *look at growth as a series of small steps taken over a lifetime.* Don't allow yourself to be overwhelmed with what you aren't doing; rather, focus on some small, new step you'd like to take today. (At the end of each chapter we will suggest some thought questions and action points to help you prioritize your ideas and move forward.) In no time these little changes will begin to make a significant difference in your relationships with your children.

Keep in mind that no matter how hard we try, most of us will never feel completely satisfied with our parenting. So make a conscious effort to redirect this dissatisfaction into steps for growth instead of occasions to become discouraged or depressed.

Third, *determine to dedicate yourself to the privilege and responsibility of fathering.* The psalmist has given us a healthy perspective on the challenge before us:

> Sons are a heritage from the LORD; children a reward from him (Psalm 127:3).

True, there are moments when all of us wonder if our children are really a reward from the Lord! But when you think that Almighty God has entrusted to us the task of preparing young lives for responsible, worthwhile adulthood, the mission takes on eternal significance. Fathering is indeed a privilege given by the Lord—a matchless opportunity to pour our lives into those we love so dearly.

As we start through these pages together, we invite you to make the commitment with us that, no matter how tough it may get, no matter how unresponsive our kids may be, no matter which way the road may bend in the future—we dedicate ourselves to the privilege and responsibility of conscientious, loving, involved, communicative fathering.

Ahead, we'll share some good tips to help you carry through.

●   ●   ●

FOR REFLECTION, DISCUSSION AND ACTION

1. Are you a full-time dad to your kids when you're home, or do you tend to remain preoccupied with thoughts of work or other things?

*2. In what ways have you noticed yourself "defaulting" when it comes to the role of parenting? What important tasks are you leaving to their mother, to their teachers, to their youth workers that really should be your responsibility?

3. Were the survey results cited in this chapter surprising to you? Why or why not?

4. What would your children state is their primary source of information about sex and sexual attitudes? Why not ask them?

*5. Do your children enjoy the close personal relationship with their father that was revealed as pivotal to healthy teen development? Why or why not?

*6. Dedicate yourself wholeheartedly to the privilege *and responsibilities* of Christian fathering. Study this book with pen in hand, underlining key thoughts and action points. Consider forming a small group of devoted dads to study and discuss these principles together.

---

*At the end of each chapter we have provided questions and action points to help you implement the principles from the chapter. If you have adequate reflection time, or if you are studying this book in a group with other men, we strongly recommend that you take the time to work through each question conscientiously. However, if time is a problem, work through the questions marked by an asterisk (*).

The Dad Definition
(Norm)

*I*t wasn't until I reached middle adulthood that I was able to establish a warm, friendly relationship with my father.

My dad's career was filled with pressures and discouragements. He had difficulty enjoying his children, and we found it difficult to approach him.

I remember placing my faith in Jesus Christ at age twelve — the first member of my family to become a Christian. But as I began to form a mental image of my heavenly Father's love for me, I couldn't help superimposing my relationship with my earthly father.

Since my dad never seemed to be satisfied with me, I felt God must feel the same way. It was as if He were saying, "Norm, why don't you straighten up? Why do I have to put up with you? You'd better get your act together, or I'm going to . . ."

You can imagine the impact this had on this young teen's self-image, let alone my misperception of the love of God! It is very common for children to think God values them in the same way their own fathers regard them. If dad is loving, warm and nurturing, they tend to picture God as loving, warm and nurturing. But if dad is perceived as cold, distant and occupied with "more important things," they are likely to feel that God is unapproachable and uninterested in them as individuals.

I had this mistaken image of God until my forties, when He brought some cirumstances my way that literally transformed my relationship with Him. I discovered what a loving, caring, vitally interested God He is! And interestingly enough, it was through these same circumstances that the walls finally came down and my father and I were able to draw much closer together than we had ever been.

As part of my fresh discovery of the nature of God, I read through the Psalms with pen in hand, noting every mention of the LORD. As I studied these verses, I realized that almost every reference provided either a direct or indirect description of our heavenly Father. I soon had several notebook pages filled with these attributes, and from them emerged a profile of what most of us would consider an "ideal" father. My conclusion? The basic qualities of fatherhood that are seen in our Lord are the qualities He desires to form in today's Christian fathers.

I had discovered a theology of fatherhood—with God himself as the role model!

Today, as I counsel with fathers, couples and families, I have found this profile extremely effective in helping men understand God's intended role for them as dads. In our own families, both Josh and I have found these attributes to be worthwhile, effective guides—as well as personal growth goals—for our relationships with our children.

A Person of Refuge

The first attribute that stood out to me from

Psalms was that *a father is one I can run to for refuge.* He is the first person I think of for protection . . . my familiar place of security. One of the most common ways David described his relationship with the Lord was to say, "The LORD is my shield, my refuge, my rock, my stronghold, my tower" (Psalms 3:3, 5:11-12, 32:7, 59:16-17, 61:1-4). No matter who was threatening him he felt no alarm as long as his Father was his protector. "The LORD is the stronghold of my life — of whom shall I be afraid?" (27:1)

What does this mean to us as fathers? This suggests that a father is one who is <u>available</u> to his children. He is a haven <u>to whom the child freely</u>, quickly and <u>naturally comes for protection and rest</u>. If we spend little quality time with our children, or if we are rude, sarcastic or indifferent when they come to us, they will not perceive us as a place of security or refuge.

Recently my daughter Jody was driving to high school in my car when she was involved in an accident. Fortunately, she was not injured; my car wasn't quite as lucky. Jody returned home, visibly upset.

I'm glad I resisted the natural urge to chastise or lecture my daughter. Instead, I hurt for her — my own child had experienced one of life's major traumas. I wrapped Jody in my arms and said, "It's okay, Hon. I'm thankful you're all right. The car can be fixed. I love you."

After about an hour, Jody went on to school. As she related the story of the accident to her friends, one asked, "What did your dad do?"

"He hugged me and told me he loved me," Jody replied.

Her friends were astonished. They assumed I would be fuming, ready to ground my daughter for two months. But on this particular day, in this particular situation, my daughter needed a place of security, not scolding or threats.

A Friend

The Psalms reveal a second characteristic of a father: *He is a warm, intimate friend.* David says, "Morning by morning, O LORD, you hear my voice; morning by morning I lay my requests before you and wait in expectation" (Psalm 5:3). Consistently we find the psalmist saying, "Lord, I can tell you anything. You are always available. You listen to my delights and my distress. You accept me for what I am. You are consistently there when I need you."

One insight from Psalm 145 has had a deep and lasting impact on my life. Verse 8 says, "The LORD is gracious and compassionate, slow to anger and rich in love." You can ask yourself, "What is a gracious and compassionate person like? What is a person like who is very patient, not subject to outbursts of anger?" Can you close your eyes and visualize such an individual?

That's what our heavenly Father is like. Motivated by grace, filled with tenderhearted feelings and consistently patient.

A Supporter

As you continue investigating the Psalms, you discover a third facet of fatherhood: *A father is one who supports his children in life's difficulties.* "The righteous cry out, and the LORD hears them; he delivers them from all their troubles. The LORD is close to the brokenhearted and saves those who are crushed in spirit" (34:17,18).

From earliest childhood we recognize our inadequacy, our weakness, our frailty. We can cope with life's difficulties when we have one in whom we can rest, rely on, find strength and seek counsel. What destroys people is being overwhelmed with problems, trials and hardships, and having no one to lean on for emotional and spiritual support.

The prophet Isaiah spoke of this quality of fatherhood. He said, "He [the Sovereign LORD] tends His flock like a shepherd; He gathers the lambs in His arms and carries them close to His heart; he gently leads those that have young" (40:11).

Bob, a young father, was telling us about his effort to help his six-year-old daughter learn to ride her bike. He ran alongside to stabilize her and allow her to learn how to balance herself. In the process, Bob accidentally let go of the bike and it crashed, sending Heather tumbling.

As he related the incident Bob expressed his own dismay at having "failed" his daughter. He so wanted Heather to trust that he would be there, that she could depend on him to support her as she learned this difficult task.

In every area of life, big or small, children need a father who provides strength for them as they take new steps of growth. The loving father eagerly participates in the child's life.

A Companion

The Psalms also point out that *a father is a joyful companion*. David prayed, "Keep me as the apple of your eye" (17:8).

Our children need to know that there is someone who is absolutely crazy about them . . . someone who enjoys being with them. Growing up with such a relationship builds a sense of inner joy and well-being. David reflects the spirit of a father when he says of the Lord,

"He rescued me because he delighted in me" (18:19). A child is more likely to have inner peace with himself and his world when he senses that he is deeply loved and cherished by his parents.

Some children rarely hear a word of encouragement or affirmation. Dan Benson, in his book *The Total Man,* tells how one survey of parents revealed that moms and dads average ten negative comments to their kids for every one positive comment. Yet, Benson observes, "experts in child psychology believe that it takes at least four positive remarks to offset the damage to self-esteem caused by one negative comment."[1]

Josh and I have heard too many adults describe the lasting hurt of never being able to measure up to their dad's expectations, the pain of never feeling the warmth of his smile, the longing for some indication of "I think you're great."

Not long ago I was conversing with one of my daughters. High school graduation was near, and she felt discouraged because many of her classmates were to receive special awards and scholarships, and she didn't expect to get any.

I didn't know what to say, but I felt prompted to put my arm around my daughter and say, "In my book you're number one." My daughter's smile and hug told me that I had said just what she needed to hear. In just five seconds' time, I had assured her that there are people who hold her in high esteem.

Present in His Child's Life

A father is also one who *is present*, and his presence is an occasion for joy. In our personal experience as well as our speaking, research and counseling, Josh and I have come to realize that a child cherishes his father's presence above all else.

David experienced this desire in his walk with the Lord. The entire 63rd Psalm speaks of his intense hunger to be with his Father because only the Father's presence was ultimately fulfilling. "My soul will be satisfied as with the richest of foods; with singing lips my mouth will praise you," he wrote in verse 5.

The parent who is going to shape his child's life is the one who is present. But the presence must be one of companionship, involvement and enjoyment. Unfortunately, statistics indicate that the 20th century American dad spends tragically little time with his children.

A Counselor and Guide

The Psalms portray a father as *the child's counselor and guide.* In every age we face unlimited problems, conflicts and decisions. Our century is marked by challenging and confusing philosophies of life. We encounter unparalleled pressure from a morally and spiritually bankrupt society that attempts to squeeze us into its mold.

In the midst of unbelievable peer pressure, a child's parents should be the first people he thinks of going to for a listening ear or for nonjudgmental help in decision-making. Usually, and to her credit, Mom is available in these times. But the child needs to know that Dad cares, too, and receive the benefit of an adult male perspective on the tough issues he faces.

David models a healthy father-child relationship in his frequent cries to his heavenly Father for wisdom in coping with the demands of life. Over and over, throughout the Psalms, he says, "Lord listen to me, speak to me, teach me your way."

One of the most important aspects of a father's guidance is in giving children spiritual direction.

Children have a right to see in their father the emerging image of Jesus Christ. They should observe in him a steady faith in God's faithfulness. Dad should have a keen interest in their spiritual nurturing and take an active role in helping them develop a love for Bible reading, prayer and Christ-centered fellowship.

Discipline also comes under this heading of guidance and counsel. The Lord, as the perfect Father, disciplines those He loves. Too often we think of discipline in a negative light . . . as punishment. We have found one definition that sure makes a lot of sense: "Discipline is guiding, educating and supervising a child's choices." As parents, dads need to be committed to helping develop the capacity for wise decision-making in their children through firm, loving and instructive discipline.

A Lens

As a result of hundreds of conversations with people seeking help with personal problems, I'm forced to conclude that few individuals have a healthy perspective on their sexuality.

At one extreme people are ashamed of it; at the other extreme they are inflamed by it. Our minds have been filled with old wives' tales, indecent jokes and tales of conquest until we cannot see our sexuality in a true light.

Our wise, loving Father helps us see the truth in this matter. Psalm 139 tells us that we have been lovingly crafted according to His perfect plan: "For you created my inmost being; you knit me together in my mother's womb. I praise you because I am fearfully and wonderfully made; your works are wonderful" (verses 13,14). Thus, our heavenly Father is the lens through which we see healthy sexuality. He helps us sort out society's distortions that threaten to deceive us about ourselves and others.

God models healthy sexuality in several ways. First, He treats us with respect and dignity. He does not use us as objects to satisfy lust, but values us as individuals to be loved and cherished. Second, Christ's sacrificial love for His Bride, the Church, is the model of how men are to love women. When He was on Earth, Jesus wasn't obsessed or controlled by His sexuality. He interacted with women graciously, lovingly and wholesomely.

Third, our Father gives our sexuality His blessing. After He created us, with all our intricate systems including our sexual natures, He announced, "That's good." One of this first charges to Adam and Eve was to "be fruitful and multiply." Our Father is not ashamed of what He has designed, but He instructs us to express our sexuality within the bonds of marital love.

Forgiving

A father is one who holds no grudges and is quick to forgive. David knew a Father who was "slow to anger and rich in love" (Psalm 145:8). The story of the prodigal son (Luke 17:11-32) is a graphic picture of the Father's unending forgiveness. His spirit is to forgive even before we ask.

Growing up is no easy task. All of us dads have to admit that when we were growing up, we made just as many (if not more) dumb mistakes as our own children. We had bad days when we were grumpy, mischievous and devilish. There were times when we just plain rebelled. Never did we stop to think that God has a way of gaining vengeance for our parents — by someday giving us children of our own, as mischievous and rebellious as *we* were!

How blessed is the child who has a father who is

patient with his sins, who is quick to forgive, who never
holds past failures over his head like a whip. This is not
to suggest that a good dad is indifferent. No, he has every
intention of instilling wisdom, godliness and maturity in
the child, but he leads him to it by love — not by anger,
rudeness, threats, criticism, or harshness.

Trustworthy

The Psalms teach that *a father is dependable.*
King David spent much of his adult life fighting battles.
He faced the enemy time and time again. In doing so he
learned where to place his confidence: "Some trust in
chariots and some in horses, but we trust in the name of
the Lord our God" (20:7). David knew that his Father
was absolutely reliable. What He said, He would do.

One of the earliest things our children learn is
whether they can trust those who care for them.
Children ask themselves, "Can I depend on those who
watch over me?" A father who commits himself to be consistently trustworthy will provide a stable environment
for his children. They will know that they can always
rely on Dad to be truthful, dependable and consistent.

When my son Joel was four years old, one of his
favorite games was when I would stand him on a stair-
way pedestal and invite him to jump into my arms.
Without a moment's hesitation, little Joel would leap
toward me, grinning ear to ear, fully confident that I
would catch him. To him, the leap was always a safe, exciting venture because he was confident Dad wouldn't
fail.

To have betrayed my son's trust would have been
unthinkable to me. I'm sure you have similar stories
with your own kids, in which they expressed a trust that
you would rather die than betray. But dads, how many
times have we unwittingly betrayed our children's trust
when they were counting on us to take them to a ball

game, or read a story to them, or listen to them without lecturing, or not embarrass them in public?

The Opportunity

As a dad, you can look upon these qualities of fatherhood as either obstacles or opportunities.

If you feel that they are an intrusion on your lifestyle or unrealistic fantasy straight from Strawberry Lane, you'll probably regard them as obstacles and hope they go away.

But if you've felt any increase in desire to make these qualities more a part of your fathering style, to exemplify the love of God to your kids by being

a person of refuge,

a friend,

a supporter,

a companion,

a dad who is present,

a lens,

forgiving,

and trustworthy,

then these qualities afford a tremendous opportunity for you to establish an effective philosophy of fatherhood.

Will you join us in a commitment to model the love and involvement of our heavenly Father to our children? We strongly believe it is a commitment well worth every bit of time and energy that may be required. For we dads will not only be giving our children a beautiful picture of God; in the process, we will also be giving them dads they'll remember as wise, caring, loving friends.

•   •   •

FOR REFLECTION, DISCUSSION AND ACTION

1. Think through the attributes of a father we have described in this chapter. To what extent have your experienced each one in your daily relationship with your heavenly Father?

2. Set aside time to thank God that He is all the things mentioned in this chapter. Ask Him to help you be these things to each of your children.

*3. On a scale of 1 to 10, rate yourself on each of the attributes of a father listed in this chapter. Be as honest as you can. Now ask your wife to rate you. (Are you feeling real bold? Ask your teenage kids to rate you!)

*4. For each attribute on which you rated 8 or below, review the corresponding section of this chapter. Write down three specific things you can begin doing this week to improve your performance.

5. If you haven't already done so, select two to four other dads who will commit to forming an accountability group with you. Study this book and work through the questions together; commit to praying for and encouraging each other toward excellence in Christian fathering.

The World
Your Child Faces
(Josh)

*T*V shows tend to reflect the values of the times.

And how those values have changed over the years! In the early sixties, the biggest problem the *Father Knows Best* family confronted was whether Kitten should get a paper route. Today, in the nineties, the typical TV plotline is whether Kitten should sleep with Tommy on the first date or wait till she "feels in love."

The world our children face is unstable, immoral and void of spiritual strength. Our society has a tragically distorted concept of morality that leads the majority of our youth to serious confusion about their own sexual attitudes. If we as parents and church leaders don't provide clear, loving and logical direction, our children will seek direction somewhere else.

One strategy that does not work is to ignore the problem, pretend it doesn't exist, or hope our kids will glide through unscathed.

On a recent trip to Florida I visited the pastor of a large evangelical church to discuss the possibility of my giving a "WHY WAIT?" message on positive reasons for waiting until marriage for sex.

Immediately, he shook his head. "Josh, we don't

need that message here. You should see our kids worship God in our praise services. They are so warm and genuine." End of discussion.

The next morning, as I sipped my orange juice in the hotel coffee shop, I noticed the youth director from that same church in another booth. I went over to introduce myself to the young man and woman with him, and learned that they were two of the key students from the church's high school ministry.

I chatted with the students for a few minutes about school and other interests. Then I asked them two pointed questions.

"Tell me, how many junior high, high school and college-age students attend your church each week?"

They looked at the youth director and ventured, "About fifteen hundred?" He nodded agreement with their estimate.

"I'm studying and speaking about sexual attitudes among our young people," I said, leading into my second question. "How many of your young people would you guess have been sexually involved—you know, have played around?"

Both the guy and the girl, without even looking at each other, blurted: "Oh, probably way over half."

I was heartbroken but not surprised. The night before, their pastor had told me, "Our kids don't have a problem with sex. I know kids in churches down the street do, but ours don't."

And I'm sorry to report that this pastor is not atypical. I have heard this response from pastor after pastor, parent after parent—well-meaning, committed Christians, wanting to be good parents, who believe that the best way to help their kids handle temptation is to act as if those temptations cannot possibly invade *their* churches or *their* families.

As dads who care, <u>our role must involve an asser-</u><u>tive effort to understand the ways of our children's world</u><u>and to help them relate to that world from a responsible</u><u>Christian worldview.</u>

Today's Child: A Profile

From our work with families and kids, both Norm and I are concerned about the way our children are being shaped by societal pressures. Our personal observations seem to mesh with those of several perceptive writers, who believe our unprecedented modern-day pressures create an environment that undermines our children's psychological health. Let's examine several of these concerns.

Problems That Come With Society

For one thing, *our children are being affected by* <u>*society's instability*.</u> Children and youth are growing up in a stress-producing environment. Unstable homes, pressure to achieve, exposure to drugs and alcohol, and rampant sexual immorality create conditions that confuse, pressure and manipulate them. We live in a transient society. This year alone 30 million Americans will move. These conditions create insecurity, instability and anxiety in their lives that can last their lifetimes.

A majority of *today's young people view the future of society with apprehension* and so have lost hope in their own future. Research shows that 68 percent of younger teens do not believe that this world even has a future, and 32 percent believe they will be directly affected by nuclear annihilation.

<u>*Our children's fears have changed drastically in*</u> *recent years.* Three years ago Nadine Brozan reported in the *New York Times* the results of a study that found the

five greatest fears of a primary-school child twenty years ago were loud noises, dark rooms, high places, dangerous animals and strangers. Today the average primary child's greatest fears are losing a parent through divorce, and being a victim of burglary, mugging, rape or cancer.[1]

One writer notes that *our society is having difficulty producing young men and women who have moral and spiritual strength to live productive, wholesome lives as adults*: "The problem is that there is a growing proportion of young men and women whose lives are marked by serious weaknesses and disorder."[2] Unhealthy sexual attitudes and behavior are part of this weakness and disorder.

After extensive research for his book, *Our Endangered Children,* Vance Packard concluded: "To me it seems clear that our society is seriously malfunctioning in its role of preparing children for adulthood. The upheaval and disarray we are seeing in childrearing patterns are unprecedented in modern times."[3] He quotes Urie Bronfenbrenner, a highly respected authority on family life, as saying that the consequences on the young are "approaching the calamitous."[4] Packard believes that the radical changes in our society have far-reaching implications for our children . . . their future, their ability to cope, their leadership in the next generation.

Unrestrained Behavior

A second characteristic of today's child is *impulsiveness — his inability to restrain his wants and desires.* One psychiatrist observed that in his early years of practice the challenge was to help clients overcome their inhibitions. Today the challenge is to help individuals restrain their impulsive desires. Much of the media emphasis is on "you deserve this," leading the viewer to believe that he should indulge himself. Thus we have a generation of immediate-gratification addicts, enslaved to their cravings.

Evidence indicates that *today's child exhibits a higher level of antisocial behavior* than the previous generation. The arrest rate of eighteen- to twenty-four-year-olds rose 1,185 percent from 1946 to 1980, but even more shocking is the fact that for those under eighteen the increase was 2,730 percent![5] Is our society fostering unrestrained behavior? The evidence suggests the answer is yes.

Generation Gaps

Third, *today's child has few adult friends*. We live in a generation of age-segmented relationships. Consequently, when a child faces a problem he is more likely to talk it over with his peers than with adults.

Many children have little or no significant relationships with adults who could model stability and provide insight and wisdom about life. When children are with adults it is usually a large-group situation where there is little or no chance to interact. They most likely are being entertained or addressed by adults, with little opportunity for close personal friendships to develop. Thus, the youngster who is looking for adult companionship, emotional support or direction is not likely to find it with adult models.

Fourth, *today's child is required to grow up too quickly*. He is exposed to adult themes too early and thus thrust into situations he is not mentally and emotionally prepared to cope with.

For example, through cable and network television our children and youth have access to movies that portray nudity, violence and foul language. Even TV series, which in the past usually portrayed the hero as clean-cut and moral, now show the hero bedding down almost one new girlfriend each week.

Some writers of children's books are exposing our kids to adult situations, believing children should not be "sheltered." Thus, "prostitution, divorce, rape and homosexual dalliance between nine-year-olds are now common in [juvenile] fiction."[6]

The World Our Children Face

When we begin to examine the society our children are facing we quickly realize there is valid reason for our concern. Without a lifestyle and value system rooted in the Scriptures, our society will continue to pursue this dangerous course.

This was vividly communicated by a recent newspaper article. The subject is teens and sex and the subtitle cries with urgency, "Statistics are too shocking to ignore." The writer says:

> The need to be liked, and therefore accepted, is ingrained into the social and cultural sensitivities of the public today through various media in a blitzlike fashion. As a result, the two forces of the need to feel important and the sexual drive take on a dynamic nature that is overwhelming to the undisciplined mind and personality.[7]

The writer proceeds to outline the stark statistics of sexually transmitted diseases and the special vulnerability of youth. He cites statistics of the rise of these diseases among children and teenagers. The thrust of his message is, "We have a serious problem and something needs to be done." Yet, he criticizes those who would teach youth to abstain from sexual activity and accuses them of making the problem more complex.

Thus, our challenge is to understand the world in which we live, discern a course of action that is biblical and then learn how to implement that course in our homes and churches. Here is the world our children share with us:

It is a society shaped by the media. Never before

have people been manipulated so powerfully by man's creative power. Listen to what those who have been involved in it say. British newscaster, Malcolm Muggeridge: "The media in general and television in particular are incomparably the greatest single influence in society today." Academy Award-winning screenwriter Paddy Cheyevsky (of television): "The most awesome, the most powerful force ever unleashed."[8]

The media gains control of our children's minds at a very early age. They are influenced not only by cartoons and children's programs, but also by equally sophisticated, cleverly designed commercials that convincingly introduce them to the world as television decides it should be. From Madison Avenue, our children learn what cereal to ask Mom for, what toys they'll die without, and what designer jeans and shoes they must wear to be accepted by their peers.

Our children are being powerfully influenced by a potent, convincing medium. Our research among 1,438 young people, ages twelve through eighteen, from evangelical denominations, indicated that these teens watched television or listened to music an average of thirty-four hours per week. Sixty-eight percent of these churched youth had attended at least one R-rated movie and 10 percent said that they had viewed at least one X-rated movie in the past six months. We cannot help but wonder what impact these sexual images have on the sexual attitudes and behavior of our kids.

It is a morally and spiritually bankrupt society. Right and wrong, good and bad have become fuzzy in 20th-century America. Our schools and media now aggressively teach that there are no absolutes. Acts that have been wrong through the centuries are now acceptable "as long as no one gets hurt." Good taste and basic decency have taken a back seat to those who flaunt sexual deviancy and obscenity in the name of the First Amendment. We sanction the slaughter of innocent unborn babies as a convenient form of birth control, labeling those who protest as the "lunatic fringe."

It is a world of sexual liberty. Our commitment to build healthy sexual identity in our children requires us to recognize the immoral thrust of today's society. Most sex education programs in public schools are not based upon abstinence, but on "acting as a responsible person."[9] In 1987 students at Dartmouth College received a "safe sex" kit at registration time. The kit included condoms, special lubricant for anal sex, various items relating to personal hygiene and a booklet on various aspects of sexual intercourse and how to make certain high-risk acts safer.[10] Many high school administrators face pressure for "safe sex" materials to stem the tide of pregnancies and sexually transmitted diseases.

Groups such as Planned Parenthood Federation of America promote sexual promiscuity under the guise of family planning. A close friend of mine in Watertown, N.Y., was planning to get married. A friend recommended Planned Parenthood as a place to get an inexpensive blood test, so my friend got her blood test at Watertown's Planned Parenthood clinic.

Afterward, she met with a PP staff counselor who emphatically stated that her marriage would be a disaster and her husband would walk out on her during their honeymoon. Needless to say, my friend immediately thought—*My blood tests!* The next few words out of the counselor's mouth were shocking: "You're a virgin, and no man will put up with an inexperienced woman." So much for "family planning."

Statistically we know that between 1970 and 1985 the rate of illegitimate births for young white women rose 300 percent. Within the black community, the problem is particularly distressing. In 1985, 60.1 percent of all black infants were born to unmarried mothers, as compared to 14.5 percent of all white infants being born to unmarried mothers.[11] Having children outside of marriage no longer carries a stigma, and for those who would prefer not to have the child, an eager abortion clinic is just a few blocks away.

The shocking (but perhaps not surprising) thing is that sexual liberty is invading the church. The "WHY WAIT?" study among churched youth revealed that they are not far behind their non-churched friends in their sexual attitudes and behaviors. We found among those surveyed that by the time they reach eighteen years of age, 65 percent had engaged in some form of sexual behavior—fondling of breasts or genitals or sexual intercourse. Of these, 43 percent had participated in sexual intercourse. A significant number of thirteen-year-olds (20 percent) had experienced some form of sexual activity. These youth could be, and are, in your church and mine.

It is a "Me" society. Our children are growing up in a society that emphasizes personal fulfillment. Books have been written to teach us how to look out for Number One. Research conducted from 1967 to 1985 among entering college freshmen revealed that today's freshmen have a greater desire to be well off financially than to have a meaningful philosophy of life.[12] The shift in values toward making money, achieving status, having power and seeking personal fulfillment has crept into homes and infiltrated the minds of parents as well. Researcher Daniel Yankelovich found that "parents expect to make fewer sacrifices for their children."[13] Thus, the concern for our own well-being jeopardizes our marriages and our relationships with our children.

It is an "addicted" society. The moral and spiritual vacuum in our land and the freedom for self-indulgence have borne costly fruit. They have produced a society that is addictive in both overt and covert ways. We are only too aware of the increase in drug and alcohol use. Drug involvement among twelve- to seventeen-year-olds increased 138.6 percent between 1972 and 1979. We are also <u>addicted to sexual pleasures;</u> consider the financial success of such magazines as *Playboy* and *Penthouse*. <u>Movies rated "G" are almost non-existent because the public demands something more sensual and sensational</u>.

<u>We are addicted to entertainment</u>. The daily average viewing time of television reflects our love affair with amusement. Sporting events are multi-million-dollar enterprises due to our spectator mentality. <u>We are addicted to food</u>. Words like *bulimia* and *anorexia* reflect eating disorders, and the success of businesses offering dieting help points out the millions who are unable to control their eating.

What This Means for Your Child

The picture we've painted in this chapter is not pleasant, but it is realistic. Our kids live in an age of great opportunities, but also of great dangers. No Christian parent can afford to be lulled to sleep with the false idea that everything's all right. We see two special implications for our children growing up in this society.

First, *without strong spiritual and emotional roots, our children will be highly vulnerable to society's values*. One specific concern we have in this book is that we not let our children be sexually exploited because of our own failure to educate them. Neither do we want to leave the formation of their lives to others who are uncaring, incompetent or ungodly.

Second, our children will live the rest of their lives in a pluralistic society. The early years of most of our lives were formed in a social order that respected Judeo-Christian values. It helped give order to our lives, even though we may have had instability in our families. The days of Judeo-Christian values guiding our society are past, and most likely will not return. Our culture does not support our biblical convictions. Our children will not see a morality in our land consistent with the Scriptures. Thus, they need parents and Christian leaders who are dedicated to model and nurture a positive, clear biblical lifestyle. Your child *can* develop healthy sexual attitudes, but these attitudes will come only as you and the Christian community you associate with prayerfully and thoughtfully build an environment in which they are nurtured.

What This Means to You as a Dad

While this chapter paints a bleak picture of the world in which our kids live, we have ample reasons to be optimistic, joyful people. After all, *our God reigns!* Daniel and his three comrades lived in an ungodly society and bear witness to us that optimism and joy can occur in any age, under any circumstances, for those whose trust in the living God is firm. Within that setting consider the following five implications.

First, *we should not assume that our children will be exempt from the pressure to conform to a destructive lifestyle* that undermines a sound sexual identity. Our civilization preaches a view of life based on hedonism and self-indulgence. It degrades and destroys one's personhood and self-respect. We will have to be diligent to guide our children through the dangers and pitfalls that surround them at every turn. Dads can view this as a challenge or a threat, but the man of God should definitely see it as a challenge.

Second, *we need a support system surrounding us and our children.* The Christian community needs to be united in ministering to its children. Parents must realize the great value in working together with others of like mind to share resources, insights and strengths. My wife Dottie and I have endeavored to do this with our

good friends, Dick and Charlotte Day, and their kids. We
try to spend lots of time together individually and as
families. We vacation together. One family tries to take
the other family's kids with them on outings and special
events.

It must be working. Recently one of Dick's sons
said to him, "If you weren't my dad, I'd want Josh to be
. . . he's a cool dude." I then asked my daughter Heather
who was the greatest dad. Her immediate reply was,
"Dick." Now that's networking!

We need all the help we can get to be good parents
today. Dads, we need each other. Children are
strengthened greatly by their exposure to other Christians who are unashamed of their commitment to Christ.
Close relationships with young adults who cherish sound
moral values provide a camaraderie that reinforces the
choices you want your children to make. If you do not
have such a support system for you and your children,
begin building one. Invite other Christians to work and
pray together with you in this worthy venture.

Third, *we must re-evaluate our priorities*. One
pressure we dads experience is busyness. In order to
prevent over-commitment, we have to decide what is
truly important to accomplish in life and focus on those
priorities. Contrary to what society may say, we can't
have it all.

Norm and I decided that we wanted to be effective husbands and fathers. We've never regretted that
decision. In fact, if we were to come to the end of our
lives having accomplished nothing else, but knew that
we had loved our wives well and nurtured respectful,
responsible children who love God with all their hearts,
we would feel that we had achieved the pinnacle of success.

Fourth, *we need to familiarize ourselves with the
specific pressures our children are facing or will face.*

Some of this comes by reading. Some comes by being alert and discerning. Much will come by *listening to our kids, listening to gain insight into their world, their feelings, their concerns.* If we win our children's love, confidence and respect they will look forward to talking to us. Dads and moms should be the first people to whom our kids turn for a listening ear, empathy and friendship.

Finally, *we need a plan.* Rarely does an individual achieve success in important areas of life without a plan. This is even more true when we face dedicated opposition to our values and lifestyle. The plan will embody the suggestions we've shared in this book; it must also be rooted in consistent prayer for our children.

If our children are to form healthy values and sexual attitudes, our plan of moral instruction and role modeling must be rooted in the nature of God, a positive view of their relationship to Him, and a commitment to respect themselves and others. Such a plan will be effective in turning the tide on society's influences.

●   ●   ●

FOR REFLECTION, DISCUSSION AND ACTION

*1. In what ways have you sensed your family succumbing to society's ideas and values? List three practical things you can do this week to help refocus on biblical guidelines.

2. What things do you see your children doing that indicate they are indeed trying to stand firm against society's corrupted value system? How have you encouraged your children in their attempts to resist the pressure?

*3. Have you and your wife worked out a plan for listening to and teaching your children the values you want them to have? If not, why not begin to formulate one now? Go through Chapters 2 and 3 and pick out three important things you want your child to know? How will you share your ideas? (Be creative — a short discussion in the car on the way to school can be far more effective than a one-hour lecture.)

Barriers to Effective Fatherhood

(Norm)

*B*eing a good man is hard.

Being a good husband is difficult.

Being a good father is the hardest task of all.

If you had a positive role model in your father, you should sing his praises to the world—and sing some additional praises to God—for the more we talk with men across the country, the more we realize that positive male role models have been more the exception than the rule.

Neither Josh nor I had that healthy male role model in our homes during our growth years. I've already shared with you about my father's preoccupation with his own life, and the general noncommunication that prevented his children from getting close to him. I remember the dark cloud that seemed to hang over me as I longed for a word of encouragement or personal interest from my father. Instead of encouraging me, though, Dad made me feel as though I were always falling short.

Josh's home situation was even more severe—his dad was a violent alcoholic. Josh can't remember ever seeing his father hug his mother. He never heard the words "I love you" directed to his mother or himself. He cannot recall ever doing an enjoyable activity together as father and son.

So when Josh was in college, before he received Christ as his personal Savior, his life was dominated by hatred for his father. He's not proud of the story, but he shares it to show (1) the extremity of his son-father relationship, and (2) how the supernatural love of Jesus Christ can invade even the bitterest heart:

"I hated my father's guts. To me he was the town alcoholic. My friends would come to school and make jokes about my father. They didn't think it bothered me. I was like other people, laughing on the outside, but let me tell you, I was crying on the inside.

"I'd go into the barn and see my mother beaten so badly she couldn't get up, lying in the manure behind the cows. When we had friends over, I would take my father out, tie him up in the barn, and park the car up around the silo. We would tell our friend he'd had to go somewhere. I don't think I could have hated anyone more than I hated my father."[1]

Fortunately, both of our stories have good endings. As I've shared with you, my father and I finally broke through to each other and we now enjoy a much closer relationship. In Josh's case, shortly after he gave his life to Jesus Christ in college, he found that he was able to genuinely say, "Dad, I love you." When his dad saw what God had done in his son's life, he asked Christ into his life, too, and never drank again. Josh's dad died from cirrhosis of the liver—his organs were too far gone from the decades of alcoholism—but he died a forgiven man, much closer to the son he had neglected so long.

Our Negative Role Models

Did you have a positive or negative male role model as you were growing up?

The reason our own role models are so important is that once we reach adulthood we tend to either react against our father's example ("I'll NEVER treat my kids that way!") or we subconsciously fall into the same patterns of fathering that bothered us so much as children.

Take a moment right now to reflect on your growing-up years. What example of masculinity did your father portray? Did he exemplify the person we see in the Psalms — a man of refuge, a friend, supporter, and companion, a dad who is present, forgiving and trustworthy?

If you were blessed with such a dad, we hope you are following his example with your own children. You can't go wrong if you do!

Many adult men are not so fortunate. Their dads may not have been self-absorbed like mine or abusive like Josh's, but their homes lacked the positive role model of God-designed maleness every child needs to see.

Some may have missed out on the dad difference altogether, growing up in a mom-only situation following a death or divorce. We tip our hats to the single mom who must be both mom and dad to her children — she has possibly the toughest task mankind ever invented.

Other men grew up in homes where Dad was absent much of the time because of long hours at work or ministry; and when he was home, he invested little time in building quality relationships with his kids.

For others, Dad was there but he made little effort to communicate. Affection and intimacy were unknown qualities. Memories of Dad are more of a sullen, silent, don't-bother-me-I'm-busy man who seemed to speak up only when angry.

If, like many of us, you didn't have a positive male role model to learn from, it is never too late to look for current role models.

We recommend that every young dad find some willing *para-parents* — a well-adjusted, loving couple who will teach you, by word and by example, what they have learned. These para-parents can provide a wholesome model for you of a man loving a woman and parents loving and spending time with their children.

Despite his lack of a positive father-model, Josh was fortunate. "I discovered two fantastic models of love: husband and wife loving each other and parents loving their children. The two models formed my image of what family and parenting ought to be.

"The first were the parents of a girl I dated for three and a half years. Paula and I had met while I was in seminary. The time I visited Paula at her home I was overwhelmed by her relationship with her folks. They actually liked each other and so respected one another. Her folks, Jim and Vivian Simpson, showed a genuine interest in their daughters and in me as their friend.

"What made being in Paula's home even more enjoyable was seeing her parents' love for each other. Needless to say, I wanted what they had in their marriage and family. I've often joked that I didn't know who I loved most, Paula or her folks.

"The Simpsons became a model, a standard, a living example to help me see what it meant for a man to love a woman and for a father to cherish his children. Although Paula and I discontinued our romance, she and her sister's continued devotion to their parents is a challenge to me to cherish my wife Dottie and my own kids the way Mr. and Mrs. Simpson loved their family."

The second model of family love came to Josh when he met fellow seminary student Dick Day, his wife

Charlotte and their four children.

"It wasn't long before I would make every excuse possible to go to their home, to be around their family, to watch them interact with their kids. I saw in their family what I wanted in my future family.

"Much of what I have learned about being a loving, caring husband and a father who cherishes and spends time with his children came from divine truth being lived out in earthly models. Even now, as Dottie's husband and as the father of four children, I continually try to observe or study other families, parents, children. Being a husband and father doesn't come easily for me, so I'll grab hold of anything that will give me a cutting edge — that means learning from others."

Perhaps you find yourself in a similar situation to Josh's when he was single. Or maybe you are already married and have children but you are struggling through the parenting process. It is never too late to learn, to grow, to develop. Look for some models of positive, effective parenting. Learn from them.

Perhaps the best place to start is in your church. By watching another man relate to his children, you can gain confidence in how to relate to your own children. Also, it is extremely important to observe how parents relate to each other. It is not just what Dad does with the kids that's important, but what Dad does with Mom in front of the kids.

Cultural Hangups About Maleness

Our 20th century culture reeks with unhealthy attitudes that trap many men. These attitudes lead them to defeat in their personal lives, marriages and opportunities as fathers. The conscientious father needs to take a hard look at what he is being taught by society and determine not to let the "system" squeeze him into its mold.

Our Definitions of Manhood

For years we have labored under the illusion that the ideal man was the <u>macho man.</u> Our heroes have been tough, brawny individuals without feelings. Often this individual consumes beer freely, dangles a cigarette from his lips and uses tough or foul language to prove his manhood. Even sports figures are often exalted because of their arrogant, I-don't-take-nothing-from-nobody attitude.

Graphically etched in our memories from the final episode of a popular TV detective program is the fact that, although the star's wife was blown up by a car bomb and it appeared his daughter had been killed, too, the star never cried. If that weren't enough, a close friend of the man was being stalked by a killer. But immediately following any distressing news the star would still be totally in control.

The longer we watched the two-hour production, the more we were impressed with the unrealistic and unhealthy portrayal of "Mr. Hero." <u>Our media heroes don't respond in a human way, which leads us to think that we shouldn't either.</u>

<u>An opposite image has emerged</u> in recent years. Television, movies and cartoons often portray men as <u>weaklings or buffoons.</u> Since the women's movement began in earnest, our media moguls have rightfully become cautious about showing women in demeaning ways. To make up for it, they seem to feel that today's men are safer targets for humor. Thus, children viewing movies and television are more apt to see men depicted as weak, foolish or immature.

<u>Why is it that if men aren't portrayed as invincible, they are portrayed as fools?</u>

Our Role Models

At a recent music festival a couple approached Josh for counseling. Their marriage was deteriorating rapidly after just one year.

The wife complained that her husband was sexually demeaning to her, and she couldn't take it any longer. At home, her husband incessantly referred to her as a whore, a bitch, etc., and told her he was going to rape her.

The husband began to weep. "That's the only way I know to treat a woman," he contested. "I can't say it any other way. It's all I ever heard from my father when he talked about or to my mother. I've tried everything to stop and I can't."

How powerful is the influence of the father model on a child's behavior!

✳ Our Work Identity

Another cultural factor that undermines the father-child relationship is a man's strong *work identity:* The first thing men ask each other when introduced is "What do you *do?*" Thus we tend to equate our vocation with our personhood.

And because of this strong work identity, many of us work longer and harder at the expense of our families because we've fallen for society's line that the only real men are those who are on a fast climb to a higher tax bracket. Upon arrival at home, we tend to forget the fact that our wives may have also had a full day at their own jobs or at home. We sit and read or sit and stare at the TV while our wives go on to prepare our meals, iron our clothes, and keep the children out of Dad's hair. "I earn the living—she takes care of the home front," is the credo that all too many dads live by, in a day when many wives are working full time in addition

to managing the home and parenting responsibilities
we've relegated to them.

When our society was more agrarian and rural,
children spent considerably more time with their
fathers. Many worked with Dad on the farm. A strong
father identity was always present. Men worked long
hours and often the family worked together. Today men
work miles away from the home, and most children know
little or nothing of their dad's vocational world. In addition, most jobs entail more mental or emotional stress.
Consequently, Dad comes home emotionally weary with
little incentive to relate to his children.

Research evaluating family life fifty years ago
reveals that the average child spent three to four hours
a day interacting, working and communicating with immediate or extended family members and other significant adults in his life. Today, that average is fourteen
and a half minutes, of which twelve are spent in negative reprimand or critique.

This issue was made real to me through a friend.
Stan and his family moved to my town to do five years
of surgical residency. I was overwhelmed by the demands
placed on Stan, Sharon and their three small children.
Stan's supervising staff demonstrated no concern for his
responsibility to his family. He worked long hours for
months at a time. He came home exhausted, with no
energy left for his children. The family assumed all this
would end when the residency was completed, but Stan's
work as a surgeon still requires long hours. He has to
discipline himself to find time for relationships at home.
Stan's situation is representative of large numbers of
men who are caught in the vocational trap . . . long, intense hours away from the family, climbing the professional ladder in quest of financial security.

Fathering is not a hobby. It is one of the most important callings a man can choose (and you *do* choose it).

When our commitment to the job strips us of time and energy to fulfill this calling, we need to reevaluate our priorities and trust the Lord to open doors for new work opportunities which are in harmony with His will.

Our View of Authority

Our society has left many men with the need to exercise *power and authority over family members.* Even prior to marriage many men see women as objects to be conquered. They often exhibit attitudes of superiority over women, believing it is their right to rule over them. Many men, because of their own father's role model or their own insecurity as a father or husband, have a compulsive need to control their environment, including their own family. Authority often is interpreted as status in a family structure and some fathers assert their authority or position in order to get recognition.

Unfortunately, many Christian men fall prey to such unscriptural thinking. The Bible teaches that the Christian husband should follow in the footsteps of Jesus Christ. We are called to "love our wives, just as Christ loved the church and gave Himself for it" (Ephesians 5:25). The biblical model of the husband/father is one who serves, rather than bosses, others.

In evaluating our attitudes toward our children, we need to ask ourselves whether we have a wrong concept of fathering. Do we approach our children on the basis of a warm, compassionate relationship, or from a position of power? Do they see us as a caring, gentle individual or a "boss" who is always giving orders and ultimatums?

Our "Loner" Mentality

American culture tends to present men as *independent, self-sufficient individuals* who blaze their own trails. Now society is trying to pressure women into the same mold. Such an attitude is contrary to the biblical call to live as a member of the Body of Christ. We are called to live out a true sense of interdependence, recognizing that we need other people. Society's view produces men who are unable to ask for help when faced with personal or interpersonal struggles.

After many years as a professional counselor, I continue to be heartbroken that wives will come willingly for counseling but their husbands often will not admit to the need. Many men view counseling as a threat to their ego. They have listened to the line that a man cannot admit to needs or inadequacies, and now they have an emotional blockage that leads them to defeat.

Our Fear of Intimacy

Many men are afraid of intimacy; yet intimacy cannot be separated from the formation of healthy sexual attitudes in ourselves and our children. Intimacy—the capacity to be real, open and honest—is a vital part of the communication network that allows biblical insights, emotional resources, sound values and psychological strength to pass from father to child.

Intimacy originates with our heavenly Father. We read in John 1:18 that "No one has ever seen God, but God the only Son, who is at the Father's side, has made him known." In the original wording, the verse speaks of Jesus being in the "bosom" of the Father.

"To be in the bosom of someone," writes William Barclay, "is the Hebrew phrase which expresses the deepest intimacy possible in human life. It is used of mother and child; it is used of husband and wife . . . when John uses this phrase about Jesus, he means that between Jesus and God there is complete and uninterrupted intimacy. It is because Jesus is so intimate with God, that he is one with God and can reveal him to men."[2]

If intimacy is desirable and appropriate between God the Father and God the Son, it must be desirable and appropriate between a father and his children. Christian men who are uncomfortable with intimacy need to view it as part of their spiritual birthright.

Our children need to feel our emotions. Few men feel free to cry. We interpret it as a mark of weakness, and we can't afford to appear weak! Like many men, I never heard my father speak of his disappointments, longings or fears. As I came to middle adulthood I realized there was a significant dimension of my dad's life that was a mystery to him. Had I experienced emotional intimacy with Dad in my childhood and youth, it would have helped me immeasurably as a father.

One famous actor said of his father, "Never once in my life did I dare venture to ask my father about his own life, let alone question his motives or conduct."

Let us put this in a positive light. Our emotions are a vital part of who we are. Increasing our capacity to share our deeper feelings with our children strengthens our bond with them. It is an expression of trust and respect. It says, "I want you to know the real me." We need to increase our capacity to lovingly touch our children; to hold them to our "bosom." We need to enrich our capacity to be warm and affectionate. These actions affirm our children's sense of security and self-worth.

One specific way we foster intimacy is through our communication. If our conversation only centers on facts and ideas, we do not reveal our inner person. Our children profit from hearing us speak of the more "inner" aspects of our life: our feelings, dreams, longings, disappointments; our personal walk with the Lord; our past life experiences and how we perceived them. *To be intimate means to share deeply, personally, openly.*

Our Embarrassment Over Sexuality

In his book *I Married You,* Walter Trobisch makes a fascinating observation. As he traveled around the world he discovered a universal embarrassment about the sexual aspect of marriage. The Africans thought the Americans and Europeans were open about it, and the Americans thought the Africans were open about it. In reality, none of them found it an easy subject to discuss.[3]

It seems to us that because intimacy has been linked to sexual relations, and sexuality embodies the richness of our total personhood, we are not only embarrassed by sex, but also by intimacy and sexuality. And men tend to be more embarrassed by it than women. Is it possible that the need to be "macho" and the need to boost our egos is a mask many men hide behind to conceal some embarrassment over our masculinity? Without a healthy perspective of our own sexuality, can we be at ease with ourselves? If we are not at peace with ourselves, can we nurture healthy sexual attitudes in our children?

Since our society has become aware of great sexual abuse among the masses, men are more fearful than ever of touching children (we are speaking here of healthy, positive physical contact). Yet if dads do not embrace their sons and daughters and thus show positive affection for them, their distancing themselves will send a negative message to their children.

I recall when my oldest daughter, Amy, reached puberty. I sensed a tendency within myself to draw back and be more reserved. At the same time I realized that Amy still needed my warmth and affection, perhaps more than ever. I decided to follow what I knew was in Amy's best interests, and not allow my uncomfortable feelings to dictate my behavior. I continued giving her hugs and expressing affection as I had before. The close relationship I now enjoy with Amy in her adulthood makes me thankful I made that choice.

One young adult woman recently shared with me how her dad seemed to suddenly quit hugging her when she began to blossom into womanhood. "As a typical egocentric teenager," she told me, "I assumed something was wrong with me. <u>It never occurred to me that my own dad would be uncomfortable because of my emerging sexuality</u>. We need to put dads at ease and encourage them to continue giving what their daughters are indicating they need—a touch of the arm, an arm around the shoulder, a warm hug—to affirm their love and devotion."

The same goes for our sons, too. They will reach an age when they feel it is "uncool" to hug Dad, but let them make that choice. Until then, in their younger years, share the same healthy hugs with them as you do with your daughters.

It's Up to Us

This chapter has focused on the personal issues a dad must face if he is to effectively nurture healthy sexual attitudes in his child.

In a society bombarded with absent, confused father role models, Dad is challenged to become a positive model for his own children.

In a society that espouses many conflicting ideas about what it means to be a man, he must sort out the distortions that he has lived with and embody a truly biblical understanding of the Christian man.

In a society that undermines a man's right to the richness of intimacy, he must maintain his commitment to be an intimate person. And finally, in a society that propagates confused and corrupted ideas and feelings about sexuality, he must rediscover the meaning of his sexuality and live it out as a healthy expression of his personhood.

These goals will not "just happen." If we are to lead our children in experiencing a full, rich life, we will have to pursue these goals ourselves. That means coming to grips with our own needs, fears and hangups.

•   •   •

FOR REFLECTION, DISCUSSION AND ACTION

This week, alone or with your group, contemplate the following questions. Give honest, in-depth answers.

1. What role model of manhood have I followed? What role model will my children follow? By observing and relating to me, what concept of manhood will my children form?

2. What cultural ideas of what it means to be a man have I adopted? In what ways do I treat women as society dictates rather than as the Bible teaches? Do I understand what the Bible teaches about masculinity and femininity? What is my attitude toward my vocation or profession—does it have higher priority than my family?

*3. How comfortable am I with the idea of intimacy? Am I intimate with my wife according to the definition of intimacy in this chapter? How intimate am I with my children? How much freedom do I have to share my feelings with my family members?

4. How comfortable am I with my own sexuality? Do I find it embarrassing to talk about the physical aspect of sex with my wife? With my children?

*5. Where do my priorities need to be modified or revised? Who or what needs my urgent attention?

Dad: The Third Greatest Influence in the World

(Josh)

*T*his year my daughter Kelly turns fifteen.

I'm going to do something I've been looking forward to for a long time. I'm going to take Kelly on a series of dates. I'll ask her out, then dress up and leave the house so I can swing by to pick her up. I'll open and close the car door for her, take her to a nice restaurant, help seat her, and initiate dinner conversation about things she wants to talk about. After dinner we'll go do another fun activity of her choice.

At the end of the evening, I'm going to lovingly tell Kelly that the way I treated her that night is the way a boy should treat her if he genuinely respects and cares about her.

My hope is that in addition to the relationship Dottie and I try to model for our kids, these dates with Dad will provide a special model for Kelly. She'll see what it means to be treated with love and respect by a date who really cares for her.

What our children see and hear from us in the

areas of sexuality and male-female relations has a profound influence on their eventual relationships with the opposite sex. I want Kelly to see the profound love and respect I have for Dottie, and I want her to carry that standard into her own dating life. I hope I am providing the husband-model that will guide her in selecting the dates, and eventually the mate, who will treat her with the same degree of caring and tenderness.

<u>A woman's capacity for intimacy—and thus her potential for successful male relationships—is directly linked to her relationship with her father.</u> A study of 7,000 women who worked in strip joints or topless bars revealed that most of the women came from absent-father homes. The researcher commented, "Most of these women conceded that they were probably looking for the male attention that they had never gotten during their childhood. Lacking that foundation, many of these women also admitted that they did not rely on men for intimacy."[1]

It seems tragic that so many women are hurt emotionally because they did not have warm, compassionate fathers to help them build strong sexual convictions. Now they wander through life seeking the completion of something intangible and elusive.

The Competition

While fathers and mothers have the first and potentially greatest opportunity to shape their child's sexual convictions, other influences provide sharp competition.

As you are already aware, the *peer group* has a formidable influence on youth. Our youth culture communicates its own message concerning personal worth, sexuality, identity and acceptance. It pressures our children to accept false values, a false sense of sexuality and a false message of self-indulgence.

We do not mean to suggest that all peer influences on our children are negative; however, the basic messages of secular young people often destroy healthy sexual perspectives.

The Greatest Influence of All

The "WHY WAIT?" teen study shows that peers are the number-one influence on our kids' sexuality— who they are as sexual beings and how they are to act sexually. However, both Norm and I believe that *the media* is the number-one influence on kids. Why? Where have the majority of their peers learned about sex and sexuality? From the media! Not from parents, not from church, not from school, not from friends—but from the steady stream of TV, movies, rock music and periodicals that are more shallow and explicit today than ever before in history.

The media, we believe, is the greatest determinant in the evangelical teenager's sexuality. Now that is scary.

What gives the media such power over young people? Consider these facts: The average preschooler spends more time watching television than a university student spends in the classroom earning a bachelor's degree. One study revealed that preschool children watch twenty hours of TV per week and grade school children twenty-two hours. "Sleeping is the only activity that commands more of their time. By the age of eighteen, they will have spent more time in front of the TV set than anywhere else, including school."[2]

Another study estimates that by graduation, the average high school student has spent 22,000 hours watching TV, which is twice the amount of time spent in the classroom during twelve years of school.

From grades seven to twelve, kids listen to an

average of 10,500 hours of rock music. The total amount of time spent in school over a period of twelve years is just 500 hours more than the time spent listening to rock music.[3] "Teenagers are inordinately influenced by the media. They have less interaction with real adults than ever before, so their friends and the role models presented in the media have an even greater impact."[4]

While we have been permissively silent, often using the media as a babysitter, they have been telling our children that their needs for intimacy and significance, as well as the cure for loneliness and emptiness, come from jumping into bed and getting it on — in other words, through casual sex or free love. But there's no such thing as "casual" sex or "free" love.

Most of our young people have developed their concept of sexuality based upon this media fiction without realizing the price tag that comes with free love and casual sex. If they are unable to revise their convictions, they eventually will pay a high price.

A young lady tells of that price:

> What the movies and the soap operas don't tell us about is the devastation and the broken hearts that occur due to affairs and premarital sex. I don't make light of the consequences of wrong sexual involvement. Without a doubt, the hardest and most painful thing I've gone through . . . more than major surgery, tests for cancer, a broken family, and numerous job rejections . . . is getting over a sexual relationship with a married man.[5]

For years now we have allowed the media to misrepresent casual sex and free love. But have we, as parents, shared with our children otherwise? Have we provided for our children the opportunity to learn God's view on sex, in such a way that they will come to realize that God says "wait" not to spoil their fun, but because He wants the very best for them?

Sad to say, most young people, even from church families, have not been able to discuss their sexuality in church. Even a greater tragedy, most churched youth have not learned about their sexuality at home. They have learned it from television, movies and music, three great influences on teens.

For the most part we have *allowed* our young people to determine who they are as sexual beings on the basis of these lies propagated by the mass media. This deception is crucial because our sexuality affects everything we say, hear, think and do. Sexuality is at the center of our human existence. Unfortunately, we have *allowed* our young people, who are growing up right now, to base their emerging sexuality and, subsequently, their adult sexual identity, on lies.

The media not only distorts sexual realities, but it also cultivates feelings of inadequacy among teen viewers. A tremendous emphasis on the value of a person is based on physical attractiveness. We are bombarded with a constant parade of beautiful men and women, giving teenagers a most unrealistic standard by which to judge their own attractiveness.

As adults, most of us realize that the media's beauty standard is not a normal one. What's more, it's constantly changing. For a time, large breasts were the standard for women. Sometimes the emphasis is on their legs or hair. Men's hairstyles have ranged from flattops to long-and-unstyled to blowdried to moussed to who-knows-what-next. Tight designer jeans used to be the "in thing," with emphasis on the buttocks. For awhile the fifties look came back.

Think what this does to the average young person. Many have a totally distorted sense of self-worth, for they determine their worth by whether they are in fashion and whether their peers accept them as being in fashion. If by comparison to the latest standards of physical beauty a teenage girl is not attractive, she sees herself as without worth or value, which results in tremendous feelings of inadequacy. If a teenage boy does not happen to match the current standards for guys, he will feel that he is unappealing and thus without value among his peers.

We all, whether kids or adults, learn best through modeling. On TV a message is communicated in the context of a real life model. Even if that message is false, after you view it for a period of time, it will become reality or truth to you, especially if you're a child.

The Environment for Nurturing Positive Values

What environment is most conducive to developing strong moral convictions in your children? What type of setting will most likely help your son and daughter develop a wholesome, well-adjusted sexuality — based on self-respect, respect for others, and a desire to honor God?

First, we know that *healthy sexual attitudes thrive where positive, visible models are present.* You, Dad, can and should be that model. Our children have a right to see warm, loving, respectful relationships between us and our wives. A father who consistently treats his wife with kindness, affirms her womanhood and cherishes her as a life partner lays a powerful foundation of emotional stability in his children.

Many years ago a young lady came to Norm for premarital counseling. He asked her if she had any fears about her forthcoming marriage. "Yes," the woman replied, "I have one great fear. I'm afraid that my future husband will gain control and rule over me. My mother said, 'I let your dad get control and life has been miserable ever since.' "

The young lady said that her mother had repeated this over and over again. "'If you ever get married, don't let your husband be the boss!' " What this young woman had seen and heard was so emotionally convincing that she not only feared it would happen, but she had grabbed control of the relationship with her fiancé and was already ruling *him* with an iron fist!

Second, *healthy sexual attitudes are nurtured in an environment where the dignity of each person is valued.* The child discovers early in life that he is respected and cherished apart from his performance. Each child is created in the image of God (Genesis 1:26) with infinite worth and value. Even James warns against cursing people because they are created in God's likeness or image (James 3:9,10).

The psalmist depicts the infinite value of God's creation: "What is man, that Thou dost take thought of him? And the son of man, that Thou dost care for him? Yet Thou hast made him a little lower than God, And dost crown him with glory and majesty!" (Psalm 8:4,5, NASB).

King David, being overwhelmed by the greatness of God and each man being created in His image, wrote: "For Thou didst form my inward parts; Thou didst weave me in my mother's womb. I will give thanks to Thee, for I am fearfully and wonderfully made; Wonderful are Thy works, And my soul knows it very well. My frame was not hidden from Thee, When I was made in secret, And skillfully wrought in the depths of the earth" (Psalm 139:13-15, NASB).

When parents have a solid commitment to the sacredness of life and communicate this to each family member, their children grow up with a feeling of personal worth. They feel secure in their personhood, their masculinity or femininity, and their personal appearance. As a result they will not usually adopt behavior that manipulates or exploits others to fill some inner void.

Third, *healthy sexual attitudes emerge in the environment that affirms and cultivates positive intimacy.* Unfortunately our society is warped in its understanding of intimacy, largely associating it with romance and sexual encounters. The media's message usually links intimacy with sexual relations. Such a limited — and often immoral — portrayal confuses children and youth, leading them to believe that intimacy can only be found within sexual relations.

A sixteen-year-old girl wrote me a letter in which she shared her struggles for intimacy and her inability to experience it. She gave a very profound, yet simple definition: "Intimacy is the capacity to be real around another person." Isn't that what we all want? Especially in love, marriage, sex and family? No barriers, no facades, no hidden agenda, just *being real.* Kids long for that with their parents, and wives hunger for it with their husbands.

True positive intimacy is the ability to take someone into your life and create an atmosphere where he also is willing to take you into his life for the purpose of building each other up according to each others' needs. An ingredient of love, intimacy is an openness to share in a constructive, positive way what our needs are whether they be emotional, physical, spiritual, sexual or financial.

Positive intimacy is where two people stand alongside each other, not independent or dependent on each other but rather interdependent with each other. The feeling is, *I have something to give to you and you have something to give to me.*

Longing for intimacy is healthy. How that longing is met is the pivotal issue. When the home is a setting for transparency, warmth, tenderness, close interpersonal sharing and wholesome affection, our children's innate need for intimacy is fulfilled. They grow up comfortable with themselves and do not need to seek a false intimacy from sexual encounters.

But it is important for the father to take the initiative in building intimacy within the home. So often it is left to the mother as "women's work." Why is it so tough for dads? Because they often have no models themselves in their own experience, and thus are uncomfortable or unmotivated to develop a natural environment of affection and mutual encouragement.

We have already observed that many young women's sexual involvement rises from a deep thirst for intimacy that should have been met in a healthy father-daughter relationship. God intended for fathers to cherish their daughters. We are speaking here of a non-sexual intimacy, the intimacy of healthy affection, affirmation, respect, positive communication. When Dad fails to nurture this in his daughter, she becomes vulnerable to other men. Not understanding the true nature of her hunger, she succumbs to men who promise intimacy in romance and sexual exploits.

Fourth, *healthy sexual attitudes emerge when children experience a secure environment.* Children are not prepared to cope with high levels of instability or insecurity. A dad who is mostly absent from his children increases the potential for his children's insecurity. When Dad is away, the children cannot experience his emotional support, his counsel or value system. Pressure is placed on the mother to meet the total needs of the child.

Like many men who have responsibilities that take them away from home, I face the issue of making sure my children feel secure at home. So I've tried to incorporate a number of practices and priorities into my schedule to help my kids feel secure in my love and affection for them:

1. I take my children with me on trips whenever possible, one at a time, and I arrange my responsibilities on the road ahead of time to insure a lot of personal time with each child;

2. I try to call home every day and talk to most of the family. I make a special effort, as time permits, to listen to the joys and sorrows of each child;

3. If I miss my son's soccer game or a daughter's special event while away, I'll ask them about the details over the phone;

4. If it's report card time, we discuss grades over the phone. I'll inform each child of my travel plans, what I'll be doing, and why I'm doing it — and I thank them for praying for me in my ministry;

5. After talking with my kids and reinforcing my love for them, I always ask to speak with their fantastic mother, the woman I love and have had the privilege of being married to for almost twenty years. Knowing Dad loves Mom is foundational to our children's sense of security;

6. As a father who is away from home 50 percent of the time, I have to concentrate on quality *and* quantity time when I'm home. So I try to reserve extra time for each of my precious kids, pay special attention to them during mealtimes, attend their school events, take them out to eat or on day trips, and let them observe how much I love Dottie by the way I regard her.

The effect of all these efforts can be very positive. Once a woman reporter came to our home to interview me for a magazine article. Even though she was writing for a Christian magazine, she followed the practice of most reporters and tried to find something negative about me that might help sell the magazine.

She turned to my son Sean, then eight, who was watching us. "What is the one thing you don't like about your dad?" she asked my young son.

"Nothing," Sean replied.

She kept prodding him, with no results. Then she smiled and coaxed, "You've got to have one thing you don't like about your dad!"

Finally, Sean came up with something. "When he goes away."

The reporter's face lit up and her expression indicated she had found a scoop that would spice up her article.

After the interview, as my guest was leaving, I mentioned that she owed it to journalistic integrity to also ask Sean what he likes most about his dad.

After some persuasion she did. Sean immediately responded, "He spends a lot of time with me."

The reporter seemed puzzled by the apparent inconsistency. I explained to her that my son's answers were what I have always desired from my children: (1) that they will never like their dad being away from them; (2) that they will always feel their dad spends a lot of time with them.

Fifth, *healthy sexual attitudes are encouraged in a setting of compassion.* Growing up is difficult for everyone. Children face criticism and verbal abuse early on. Schoolmates can be vicious in their ridicule and name calling. It is a time of competition and pressure to achieve. How easy it is for a child to feel like an outsider, a failure, a misfit, an ugly duckling!

When a child can return to the safe harbor of his home and find warmth and compassion from a wise, empathetic, listening parent, he renews his strength. The attacks on his worth, personhood and identity are ministered to; healing, insight and strength enrich the child's developing personhood.

Compassion is not only important for those in the home, but our compassion for others outside the home demonstrates the infinite value God places on individuals. One morning as my children and I were leaving the Rongbranch Cafe in our small California hometown, a man approached us. He told me about the hard times that had fallen upon him, and about his need for a job and some money for food. My son Sean and one of my daughters, Katie, watched as I tried to encourage the man. Then they followed me into the cafe.

Inside, I gave the waitress enough money for three hearty meals from the menu. I told her to give the man any three meals of his choice that day, then give him any money left over — and to please not say where the money came from.

As we returned to the car, Sean said, "Gosh Dad, that was neat," and gave me a big hug.

Several months later we were vacationing in Mexico. While we were sightseeing, Katie looked thoughtful. "Daddy," she asked, "could I do some work — you know, to earn some extra money?"

"Why?" I asked. "What would you use the money for?"

Her little blue eyes sparkled as she pointed to several hundred decrepit shacks on a hillside. "I want to take it up there and give it to all those people just like you did for that man at the restaurant."

It was thrilling to see how one little act of compassion at a restaurant would motivate a child to feed a village. Such compassion, openly practiced among family members as well as other human beings, demonstrates to our children that we are to *love* people and *use* things — a philosophy that will lend immeasurable integrity in their future human relationships.

Today's media, and its accompanying peer pressure, is tremendous competition for our children's system of values. But our research and experience shows that a well-adjusted, involved, loving dad can wield a powerful influence in his own right. So don't default, fellow dads. Let's not forfeit our kids to society's distorted pictures of manhood and womanhood, beauty, and interpersonal integrity.

Norm and I strongly encourage you to make every effort to create in your home life an environment that provides your kids with positive role models, respect for personal dignity, positive intimacy, personal security and compassion. We have found this environment to be essential in guiding children toward a responsible, caring adulthood that honors Jesus Christ.

● ● ●

FOR REFLECTION, DISCUSSION AND ACTION

1. What kind of influence do you think the media are having on the sexual values and self-worth of your children? Be specific.

2. Review the five environments where healthy sexual attitudes are developed. Identify two specific areas where you would like to see improvement in your home, and tell what you intend to do to begin nurturing these areas.

*3. Besides earning a living, what specific things are you doing as a dad to help each of your children feel secure in your love and affection? From reading this chapter, what ideas did you underline that might help you do better in this area?

*4. Have at least two "Dates with Dad" with each of your children during the next six weeks. Plan something they want to do, then devote your full attention to them during the date. Make it fun — for both of you!

Building a Quality Relationship

(Norm)

*F*or the past several years I have made a point to have breakfasts with my children, one each week, at a local deli. These are times of friendly conversation that we will always cherish.

Recently Jody told one of her friends at school that she and her dad had gone out to breakfast that morning. Her friend responded, "Oh, are your parents divorced?" She was surprised to find that a father and daughter would choose to enjoy time together as a part of normal family life.

The Success Equation

We often tell parents, "If we could give you only one guideline for parenting it would be this: Build a quality relationship." Successful parenting is based on the quality of the parent-child relationship.

Since we are looking at the roots of healthy sexual attitudes in our children, perhaps this simple equation will help you to see why the quality relationship is vital.

Warm Compassionate Dad	+	Quality Relationship	+	Impressionable Child	=	Healthy Sexual Attitudes

Obviously many other elements contribute to healthy sexual attitudes in our children, but without the strong father-child relationship, they are bound to be less effective. For Josh and me, maintaining and enriching our relationship with each of our kids has borne fruit in their lives — and in our own. We are both thankful to be able to say that our children are among our best friends.

My wife Winnie and I were invited to a friend's home for the evening. Tom and Janet were excited that Tom's brother was expressing interest in Jesus Christ. Dave had attended a family life seminar that ministered to his needs, then several other circumstances had seemed to add to his awakening spiritual interest.

"One thing worries us," Janet said. "Dave's neighbors are Christians, but what they portray is very negative. They leave trash on their lawns. Their children are mean to Dave's child. And the husband and wife seem very insensitive. We're praying that their example won't turn Dave off from the Lord."

There's an important principle here: The ideas, attitudes and behaviors we exhibit toward others either draws them to us or repels them away from us.

During his earthly ministry Jesus consistently drew people to himself. One incident that has imprinted itself on my mind is Jesus' interaction with the Samaritan woman at the well (John 4). He made a simple request: "Give me a drink." Immediately the woman sensed a spirit in Him that was different from the other Jewish men she had known. Evidently others had been rude, insulting and demeaning . . . men who had "turned her off." As her brief conversation with Jesus Christ unfolded, *she was drawn to Him.* When she left his presence she hastened back to her village and excitedly told others about this amazing person she had just met.

So *the simple fact of relationships is that certain habits, attitudes and behaviors attract people to us and others drive people away from us.* If we, as dads, want to have a significant influence on our children's lives, then we need to ask ourselves: "Which attitudes and actions will draw my child to me and which ones will undermine our relationship?" This principle gives us practical ways to build, maintain and enrich our relationships and increase our power to communicate Christ's love to our children.

Practicing the Principle

There are several practical ways we can strengthen relationships with our kids. Think through the questions that follow. You'll find suggestions which either reinforce what you are already doing or give you new ideas you can put into practice. Think of specific ways to apply any insight you gain.

What draws my children to me and what drives them away from me?

This question helps you evaluate: (1) your existing actions toward your children, and (2) your children's likes, dislikes, personalities and development.

Recently a teenager shared how his dad's behavior had really upset him. The boy was at that awkward stage when he wanted to ask a girl for a date but found it embarrassing to do. It seemed as though whenever he mustered the courage to make the phone call his dad was around. Dad found pleasure in making faces and ribbing him while he was talking on the phone.

However cute and innocent that behavior may have seemed to the father, it was driving a wedge into his relationship with his son. Dad was making it very difficult for his son to come to him to talk about his difficulty in relating to girls. This was especially sad since the father loved his son and had many good insights to share with him. Yet this persistent behavior hindered, instead of helped, the relationship.

All sorts of behaviors can create barriers to a good relationship with your kids:

● Consistent criticism

● Being too busy when they seek you out

● Making promises and not keeping them

● Wanting to do things with them that hold little interest to them

● Betraying confidences

● Prejudice

● Sarcasm

● Teasing

● Ridicule

Why not pause for a minute in your reading and make a list of behaviors that turn off your child? What does an individual his age dislike? Is there anything your child has asked you to stop doing? What has your wife shared with you that she observes? Ask both your child and your wife for their honest input.

At the same time, it's just as important to identify the positive behaviors that attract your children to you. People are more likely to be attracted to a person who:

● Smiles and is optimistic

● Is affirming and complimentary

● Takes interest in that person's interests, talents and ideas, and

● Is available.

Why not take time now to make a list of those specific behaviors that attract your child to you. Again, ask your child. Ask his mother.

What do I think about my child?

Our underlying attitudes toward our children will influence our conversation and actions toward them. For example, if we think that children are a necessary evil to be endured, our actions cannot help communicating the message, "I have to put up with you, but I don't like it. I'm glad when I can return to relationships with adults—the really 'fun' people." By contrast, thoughts guided by the biblical idea that "Sons are a heritage from the LORD, children a reward from him" (Psalm 127:3) communicate delight in being with these "gifts." Our attitudes and actions express how much we enjoy God's special gifts . . . our children.

Remember, *attitudes lead to actions.* What messages am I sending to my children? Are my messages (both words and actions) attracting my children to me like a bear to honey or driving them away like smoke in the eyes?

The participants of a parenting seminar were asked to name one new thing they would like to do the following week as parents. One father spoke up. "I'm going to go home and treat my children as nicely as I've been treating the neighbor's children." He had identified an attitude that was defeating his relationship with his children.

How much time am I spending with my child?

As mentioned earlier, the studies of father/child relationships indicate that most fathers spend very little time with their children. Yet time is one of the greatest gifts we can give. *Most children equate love with time.*

Jim, a successful stockbroker in his own right, hardly knew his father, who had spent long hours at the office. When his father died, Jim and his wife came into a significant inheritance. But Jim's only comment to me was, "I would give it all back to have five minutes with my dad."

Jesse was vice-president in charge of construction in a huge international conglomerate. His wife, in a conversation with Josh, shared that her husband had made millions and had been extremely successful at his job, but as a father he had been a total failure. None of his six children came to visit him before he died, she said. His dying comments were that he would gladly give up his millions and accomplishments in business to be a successful father and have the devotion and respect of his children.

I am thankful that I learned this lesson when my children were very young. Once, when my family was eating lunch on a Sunday afternoon after church, I said to the kids, "I'm going to give each of you a gift today." Their eyes lit up with eager, inquisitive expressions.

"I'm going to give each of you thirty minutes. I'll do whatever you want to do during that time." Their response was a squeal of delight as energetic as if I had presented an attractively wrapped package.

I asked Amy what she would like to do. "I want to go for a walk with you, Daddy." So we walked through our neighborhood, hand in hand, and stopped for an ice cream cone.

When we returned home Joel indicated that he wanted to wrestle on the front lawn. So we wrestled for thirty minutes.

Then I asked Jill, who was preparing to enter kindergarten, what she wanted to do. "I'd like to sit on your lap on the back porch lounge chair and have you read to me." So we read.

That afternoon I learned how significant the gift of time is to our children. When it is given eagerly and generously, it pays rich dividends.

Can I see what life looks like through my children's eyes?

We cannot help being drawn to the person who takes time to understand our ideas, our problems, our joys and our dreams. The individual who can empathize with others is very attractive. Perhaps we dads need to look at life through our children's eyes for a change.

To help me gain this perspective, I like to ask, "What does life look like for . . . ?"

- the child who is failing math and who is receiving constant criticism but little help;
- the child who has difficulty establishing friendships;
- the child who wets the bed and can't get control;
- the child who feels athletically incompetent;
- the child who feels ugly;
- the daughter who seldom gets asked on a date;
- the son whose friend has just rejected him;
- the child who is being ridiculed because he's a Christian;
- the child who has been unfairly punished by his teacher.

One skill we all need to learn as caring dads is that of perspective-taking—the ability to intellectually *and emotionally* grasp how our children perceive and feel about themselves, others, their circumstances. Hours in counseling situations have taught me that everyone seeks someone who cares enough to understand how life looks through their eyes. Think about your children for a moment. How does life look to them? Can you remember what it felt like to be their age? (Take the deepest emotions and strongest temptations you felt as a child and multiply by at least ten. This may give you just a hint of how it feels to be a kid in today's culture.)

Do I cultivate mutual interests with my child?

Living separate lives is easy; building bridges that are strong and allow us to travel back and forth into each other's lives takes work. But we think you'll find it well worth the effort.

Mutual interests help build those bridges and make relating a pleasant, fruitful process. Without common interests we have less basis for sustained contact in our families. The wise parent begins to build mutual interest with his children by getting interested in their world. When children are young, the hours spent in play bind parent and child together and establish the foundation for later relationships.

The parent who reads to his small children in their early years builds a point of contact to share books and ideas in later life. It thrills me whenever my grown children come to me now and say, "Dad, here's a book I've been reading I think you'll really like." My son Joel recently brought home one of Charles Colson's books. We're reading it at the same time, and it gives us yet another subject to discuss together. I feel honored when my daughter Jill asks me to listen to a new cassette tape she has purchased.

Josh has discovered the joy of mutual interests, too. He recently found himself sitting in his son's classroom, where Sean was selling pizza at his class fair and wanted his dad to see his fast-food operation. When Kelly won first place at the San Diego science fair, Josh volunteered to take her and two other winners to the state science fair in Los Angeles for three days. He exhibited interest in Katie's world by going to her open house at school and admiring her projects. He enlisted Kelly's help in selecting his wardrobe for fifteen TV specials—

the tapings called for twelve changes of clothes, all of which would appeal to teenagers and would not be out of style in five years!

What do you and your children share in common? How have you shown your kids recently that you are interested in their latest projects? Is there something you can do this week to build a bridge between you and your children?

In Search of Intimacy

An interaction occurs between intimacy and relationship. Intimacy is the closeness that occurs as a relationship develops and deepens. It is the feeling that this person is special to me and I to him. We hold each other as beloved in our heart and can share personal issues . . . even secrets . . . that are important to our lives.

We may share *intellectual* intimacy—ideas, discoveries and values that we cherish. Or, our intimacy may be *emotional*—the feelings we hold that are very personal, that others do not know about. Intimacy may be *social*—spending time with mutual family members and friends we are close to and care about. We may share intimacy around *goals* that bind us together—those dreams that are very personal, those ambitions we unitedly pursue. Many people also discover intimacy in *crisis*, because going through crisis times together often creates an understanding and companionship that was not present before. Last, there is *physical* intimacy that includes sitting side by side, engaging in verbal and physical expressions of affection and, within the commitment of marriage, sensual touches and sexual intercourse.

These various expressions of intimacy are mentioned because all, with the obvious exceptions of sensual touching and sexual intercourse, need to find their way into a dad's relationship with his children. Each dimension is a viable channel for forming a positive self-image and a healthy perspective on what it means to love others as yourself. Our children long for multifaceted intimacy with us and they thrive on it when it comes forth from a loving parent. Building a warm, positive relationship allows this to emerge.

Let's ask a final question before we conclude this chapter. How does father-child intimacy foster healthy sexual attitudes?

Intimacy opens doors and windows through which your children perceive your own feelings about your personhood. It gives them insight into your thoughts and feelings about yourself, your thoughts and feelings about the opposite sex and your understanding of your own sexual role in marriage and the family.

Intimacy provides Dad the opportunity to affirm his child's sexuality. His daughter feels cherished, valued and respected. Dad's affirmation and affection fills her emotional tank, leaving her free to pursue life in a wholesome manner. His son feels trusted, loved and admired. He doesn't have to "prove" he is a man. Intimacy nurtures healthy self-image, which nurtures healthy sexuality, which nurtures healthy sexual attitudes.

Intimacy also opens the door for meaningful conversation. When children feel close, accepted, valued and respected, they feel safe in expressing uncertainties, fears and problems they are encountering. We as fathers then have the joy of walking alongside our children as they process these issues. They know they are not alone, and this knowledge gives them strength.

In his book, *My Beautiful Feelings*, Walter Trobisch shares correspondence he had with seventeen-year-old Ilona. She had written him concerning her sexual struggles. At one point she described her relationship with her father. Listen to her comments:

My father is a businessman and is seldom home. Even when he is there, we rarely talk together, just the two of us. I am sure he means well and tries to take good care of his family. When I was small, I often sat on his lap. But during the last few years he has stopped touching me at all. Sometimes I think that he is afraid of that. Don't misunderstand me: We don't quarrel with each other. I certainly can't say that we have a bad relationship. I'd rather say that I don't have any relationship with him. I feel distant from him.[1]

Later in her letter Ilona told about a boyfriend. They would go out for walks. Ilona wrote,

The third or fourth walk ended with embracing and kissing on a bench in the park. That was my first experience of this kind. I didn't even try to stop him *because I had been longing for something like this for a long time.*[2]

The connection between her father's behavior and her behavior with her boyfriend is obvious.

By contrast Donald Heinz describes his positive experience with his family relationship that fostered intimacy and met his needs:

Mostly I recall a feeling of security, and emotional warmth in our "interpersonal relations" in the family. Lots of singing, lots of verbalization of feelings (before people wrote books about the necessity of that), lots of physical contact: kisses, hugs, lap-sitting, handshakes, and embraces— [even] when I thought I was too old for kisses. "Go to your room" was a command I never heard, though spankings were certainly not unknown. We weren't a family where parents and children separated after the evening meal to leave each other in peace, except, of course, when we went out to play. We were a lot of sunshine for each other, I think.[3]

In Search of a Father Figure

Over the last several years Josh has seen a distinct change in the way he is perceived by high school and college students. Several months ago he was sort of puzzled; he seems to be more effective with kids now that he's in his early fifties than he was fifteen years ago. At one conference a group of ten to twelve high school students approached him. They exclaimed, "Everyone here really loves you!" Needless to say, every speaker likes to hear that.

But his earlier thoughts about age and effectiveness immediately caused Josh to ask, "Why?"

One of the guys answered, "We've been talking about that, and we've concluded that you are the kind of father we've all wanted to have. We've been watching you and your kids all week."

Josh reflects, "It wasn't my messages, it wasn't my humor, it wasn't my insight into teenage problems, but rather my relationship with my own kids. The two most frequent comments I get from kids today are 'Will you give me a hug' and 'I wish you could be my dad.' Kids need to be hugged, and to know they are special. Dads, if they don't feel loved and special at home, they will look to their peers to satisfy that need."

Kids are responding more to Josh now because he is a father figure to them. It seems that most kids will respond better to someone they admire as a father rather than to an authoritative figure or peer. Are you a father your kids can admire?

Your kids want you! We pray that you will have the joy of introducing your sons and daughters to the important issues of life, to shape their views of and feelings toward themselves. You will never have a greater opportunity to sustain a life-long, intimate relationship with someone. The power of what passes between you is largely determined by the strength of the relationship.

We hope you feel as challenged as we have been to build and maintain a warm, strong, affirming relationship with our children — for life.

• • •

FOR REFLECTION, DISCUSSION AND ACTION

*Read through the following situations. Ask yourself, "Is this typical of me?" Use your answers to help you evaluate your relationship with your child.

1. Immediately after dinner Dad leaves the table to watch television or read the newspaper.

2. Dad believes children should be cared for by their mother.

3. One of the children comes for help with school work. Dad lays aside the newspaper and is eager to be of help.

4. This week Dad spends only twenty minutes with his daughter, though he plays golf, watches television, and reads the newspaper.

5. Dad looks forward to spending time with the children at bedtime. He sees it as a great opportunity to read to them and have warm, personal time.

6. His son wants to sit on his lap but Dad shoves him off.

7. When his daughter tries to give him a hug, Dad seems embarrassed.

8. At the supper table one of the children starts to tell about an incident that happened in class. Dad is disinterested and changes the subject.

9. Dad often talks with his son about his own childhood. He mentions his own insecurities as a boy and shares how he coped with them.

10. When his six-year-old daughter talks about her boyfriend, Dad makes fun of and teases her.

The Dad Who
Communicates
(Josh)

A successful businessman, unhappy about his
relationship with his eighteen-year-old son, recently came to Norm's office for counseling. The boy was unmotivated, involved in drugs, and had established
destructive friendships. Communication between father
and son was strained.

Norm suggested that the father take his son to
lunch the following week. "This is not a time to chastise
or preach to him," Norm explained. "Your task is to communicate friendship. Express an interest in him. *Listen.*"

When the businessman returned the following
week he described the event. "How did your son
respond?" Norm asked.

"Well," the dad began, "he said that all during
the lunch time he kept waiting for the shoe to drop!" The
son had expected his dad to correct or reprimand him because that was what had happened in all the other situations. Unwittingly, the well-intentioned father had
previously established a communication pattern of consistent criticism and condemnation.

Nearly a quarter century ago Walter Stokes
wrote about the importance of good communication be-

tween parent and child:

> As the author has perceived it, the master cause of poor parent-child relations and of poor preparation of children for adolescence lies in the *creation by parents of insurmountable barriers to honest, unafraid, adequate communication with their young people.* If children can arrive at adolescence with even a modest affection and respect for their parents and a fairly good ability to communicate with them about all things, adolescence will be taken in stride and without dramatic difficulties (italics added).[1]

The Key to Good Relationships

Effective, positive communication between parent and child produces healthy relationships. Too often, though, communication channels are never opened, or at some point barriers are erected that limit or completely block the exchange of information and feelings.

When communication channels are closed, several unfortunate consequences follow: possibilities for a satisfying relationship cease, resources to enrich each other cannot be shared, the delight of companionship and teamwork are not experienced, and the provision for healing when hurt or misunderstanding occurs cannot take place.

The weight of positive influence we exert on our sons and daughters will be directly proportional to the kind of communication pattern we use. If we are serious about guiding them to responsible perspectives on life, we need to examine the kinds of interaction that transpire between us. We hope that this chapter will prompt self-examination and give you a vision of the power and promise of an affirming approach to communication.

The Positive Dad

When we dads stop to think that parents average ten negative comments to their children for every positive comment, we may wish to monitor our own communication patterns. Most dads, no matter how spiritual or conscientious, find that indeed they are more prone to send messages laced with criticism, commands or demands.

Our incentive for being positive dads comes from the Bible. The apostle Paul admonishes us: "Let no unwholesome word proceed from your mouth, but only such a word as is good for edification according to the need of the moment, that it may give grace to those who hear" (Ephesians 4:27, NASB).

What we say usually falls into one of two categories: (1) destructive, critical and unwholesome communication; or (2) positive, affirming and edifying communication.

Suppose you and I are in the same room. You recognize me and decide to introduce yourself. You walk up to me, extend your hand and start to say, "Hello, Josh, I'm . . . " Before you can utter the words, I reach out and slap you hard on the cheek! You are startled, hurt and confused at my odd behavior. For a few minutes you stand in the corner pondering what to do. Finally, you decide to try again. However, you proceed toward me more cautiously this time, watching for signals from me. Again my hand darts out to strike you. *How many times will you continue to approach me?*

Our words can be as vicious as our hands! Words hurt. Words leave wounds. If we lash out at our children with criticism, sarcasm, bossiness, we will leave behind damaged lives.

For the positive side, let's look at this truth in a different light: Positive communication is equally powerful for good. Our words can be God's way of strengthening our children. They can be vessels that carry encouragement, hope and life. Our words can give grace to our children (Ephesians 4:29).

Are we committed as fathers to being positive influences on our children? Are we committed to speaking to each of them with nurturing, encouraging, enriching words? *Even problem situations can be handled with a positive approach.* Because our children are disobedient doesn't mean that we are justified in resorting to ugly, belittling and condemning language.

The affirming father builds confident manhood and womanhood in his sons and daughters through his words and actions.

The Listening Dad

Another important aspect of communication is *listening.* When speaking we can send positive messages; when listening we can extend empathy and compassion. We can become sounding boards, helping our children process their own thoughts and feelings.

Norm learned the importance of being a listening father many years ago: "My son Joel (at that time an eighth grader), came home from school in an irritable mood. I was in my den and heard him slamming doors and speaking rudely. At the dinner table he was cranky and sarcastic. Later in the evening I was in my den and again heard him angrily slam the door to his bedroom.

"Finally the glaring light went on in my mind: *Something important must be bothering Joel.* For the past four hours he had been visibly upset. I went to his room and said, 'Joel, I just realized that you came home in an irritable mood. Is there something that happened at school that you'd like to talk about?'

"My son began to weep (and frankly, I felt like a

dummy for not seeing the problem sooner). He poured out his hurt concerning an incident that had happened in the classroom. He had been embarrassed and misunderstood by a teacher. Not knowing how to process it, he carried it home and it kept leaking out in his negative behavior.

"What my son needed that afternoon was a dad who could empathize with him, one who would listen, one who recognized that boys experience painful situations, one who would not belittle him. I'm thankful the message got through to me."

The listening dad lets his children know there is someone to whom they can turn to find refuge . . . someone who is loving, accepting and supportive. He says by his actions and attitudes that there is a resource available to them, that they don't have to go through their problems alone. The listening dad is a picture of how the heavenly Father is always available to listen, encourage, strengthen and forgive.

The Warm, Gentle Dad

Communication experts remind us that communication involves far more than the words we speak. Some say our words make up only seven percent of our communication. Thirty-eight percent comes from our voices (pitch, speed, intensity, inflection); 55 percent is non-verbal (gestures, posture, emotions).

This raises an important question for us as dads: *What non-verbal messages are we sending our children?* This just might be the most important message of all. My non-verbal messages may color my words so thoroughly that what I think I'm saying isn't what my child hears. My intent is to be a loving father, but my body language and mannerisms may be saying, "I don't want to be bothered with you."

What does a warm, gentle, yet firm person look like? The best picture we have of such a person is Jesus Christ. He said to His followers, "Come to me, all you who are weary and burdened, and I will give you rest. Take my yoke upon you and learn from me, for I am gentle and humble in heart and you will find rest for your souls" (Matthew 11:28,29). Jesus models the warm, gentle, firm man we are all challenged to become. He says of Himself, "I am the resting place for the weary and burdened. I am a gentle and humble person." Needy people flocked to Christ. They found in Him one who was compassionate, who genuinely cared about their diseases, disfigurements and discouragements.

Let's face it, our society doesn't teach us to be warm and gentle men. John Wayne gets the spotlight, not Jesus Christ. The characters played by Chuck Norris, Clint Eastwood and Sylvester Stallone are our typical American heroes, tough and without feeling.

But our children need fathers who are like Jesus — men with backbone, but who are also tender-hearted and approachable. They need fathers like the apostle Paul, who said of himself, "[I was] gentle among you, like a nursing mother caring for her little children" (1 Thessalonians 2:7). Such fathers have a profound positive influence on their children. Their approachable manner creates an open door through which children freely discover friendship, wisdom, affection and security. Such fathers offer the rich inner strength of character, not mere physical brawn.

You may be saying, "Josh, Norm, you don't understand. All my life I've been taught to be tough. I was told not to share my emotions. That's a sign of weakness. Now you're saying to me that I need to be tenderhearted, gentle and compassionate. That frightens me."

One of the wonderful benefits of fatherhood is that it challenges and motivates us to grow. In our fatherhood we discover where we are inadequate, where we've been misdirected and where we need God's Spirit to liberate and empower us. *We can anticipate that our Father will use this crucial relationship to motivate us to growth.* Thus, rather than fearing the challenge before us, we honestly need to look forward to the liberation of becoming fully man, which is all that we are intended to be through Christ. God will empower us to take little, sometimes faltering, steps throughout the rest of our years as He forms us into His image.

The Transparent Dad

Children face many struggles as they grow up. If the adults they follow appear perfect and infallible like gods, children may see themselves as inferior and may perceive their struggles as evidence that something is wrong with them. Living among the gods can be very intimidating. Our children need relationships with adults who are capable of appropriate transparency.

Transparency can be either appropriate or inappropriate. *Inappropriate transparency* involves self-disclosures that are detrimental to children. The father who constantly berates himself, condemns his own actions as stupid or repeatedly recounts all his failures is practicing inappropriate transparency. He models low self-esteem, which in turn fosters insecurity in his children. The children see their father as incompetent and not one to turn to in time of need.

Appropriate transparency allows the children to see inside their dad. They hear their father talk about his own experiences as a child and youth. They discover how Dad perceives himself, his masculinity, his role in life. They grasp their father's perception of the opposite sex — what his thoughts are about Mom, about women in general, about sex, love, marriage, commitment, and most importantly about himself.

A common problem many men face is their inability to express their feelings. In essence, we *learn* to express or suppress our feelings. When Dad feels free to talk about his joys and disappointments and his fears and longings in a healthy way, his children gain a more complete view of manhood. Men who possess healthy openness about their emotions form closer ties with their children.

Through the father's openness about his own life, his children come to understand how a responsible adult male copes with life. When they face similar situations they are more confident because they have learned that problems are a natural, healthy aspect of the process of maturity. As Dad shares how he copes with his problems and challenges, his children gain insight that is valuable in their own experiences.

The Available Dad

Meaningful communication takes time. Often, time for family relationships gets squeezed out by the tyranny of the urgent. The conscientious dad guards his time with his children and refuses to let other commitments and pressures take control of his life.

I find that I need to pencil in and plan dates with my kids. Often we'll meet right after school for about an hour. I have to constantly remind myself that this is special time with that specific child, and I try to put out of my mind any book I'm working on or talk I'm preparing. If people stop me on the street to talk, I try to graciously keep the conversation brief so I can continue to give undivided attention to my child.

Once I was at a crucial point in finishing a manuscript to meet a deadline when Sean approached me. Without even letting him speak, I said, "Not now, I've got to finish this manuscript." My disappointed son had no sooner left the study than Dottie entered the room and boldly, in love, confronted me: "Honey, you're always going to have deadlines, but you're not always going to have a seven-year-old son wanting his daddy's time."

She was so right! Without a moment's hesitation I put down my pen, pushed the large, comfortable chair away from the desk and hurried to find Sean. What an invaluable lesson for a busy father in setting priorities!

Once we determine to set aside ample time for our children, we need to plan how that time can be used to foster significant communication. We have found that the quality of communication improves when we remove distractions. A thirty-minute walk in the neighborhood usually creates the setting for an enjoyable, meaningful talk. We are more likely to release other problems and tasks from our minds and become more sensitive listeners. Going out to breakfast together places you in a face-to-face setting, with other family members out of the scene.

When time is reserved for our children, we need to be careful that it doesn't become a time to straighten them out. Save your lectures on their behavior for another time. Some basic guidelines for these planned times together could be: (1) listen to your children, (2) share with them from your personal world, (3) be available for any counsel or insight they may be seeking.

Every relationship will be unique. A few years ago Norm and his daughter Jody decided to restore a 1964 Triumph sports car. Jody didn't mind a bit that the grease and oil got under her fingernails, that a few nails actually got broken, and that rebuilding brakes and knocking out dents is tough work—it was a special time with her father each week as they worked together toward a common objective, with lots of conversation and laughter mixed in. The experience provided a delightful context for communication and learning.

Your relationship with each child should have its unique flavor, which will give you special opportunities to share important dimensions of your life.

The Sexual Dad

The communication process between father and son or father and daughter is essential if your child is to profit from you in his pilgrimage toward healthy sexual attitudes and behavior.

You and your wife have the first and best chance to guide your child toward personal wholeness. If open and positive communication channels are maintained, the richness of your own sexual security will color the relationship. Your son will learn from you what it means to be a man and how he should treat a woman. He will feel comfortable about himself because he has had one of the best guides available. Your daughter will gain self-respect and cherish her femininity as she hears you express your delight in her. As she grows older she will have a sound basis by which to measure other men with whom she relates. She will be less vulnerable to the exploits of men because the authority of your life and love will provide a defense. She will learn how to relate to those of the opposite sex.

Your ability to express and talk about the sexual aspect of your personhood is a vital element in your relationship with your children. We can learn a lesson about discussing personal purity and sexual morality with our children from the Bible. In Proverbs 3 through 7, children are instructed to listen to the wisdom of their parents about sexual matters. The parents are never admonished or commanded to talk to their children about sex. It is assumed that the parents *will* talk to their children. Have you followed through on communicating with your children about this very important part of their lives?

There are several excellent resources available for parents who need help in this area. One book we heartily recommend is *Talking With Your Kids About Love, Sex and Dating* by Barry and Carol St. Clair, who give step-by-step guidance to moms and dads in discussing these subjects at their children's various age levels. Another helpful resource is the attractive gift set of three books I edited for teens: *Dating: Picking (and Being) a Winner; Sex: Desiring the Best;* and *Love: Making It Last,* written by veteran youth workers Barry St. Clair and Bill Jones. A home video resource is *Let's Talk About Love and Sex.* This video is designed with an accompanying book to give to your young teen after watching the video together. The book, *Love, Dad,* is a collection of letters I wrote to my son and daughter on how to handle the sexual pressures and temptations they would soon be facing.

The importance of communication in the area of sexuality raises one issue you need to face. If you are uncertain or uncomfortable with your own sexuality, you will communicate this to your children. If you were raised in an environment that belittled women, you may communicate attitudes and feelings to your daughters that will leave them vulnerable to men. If you were taught that men are to be strong, silent, tough and insensitive, your sons may pick up these same tendencies by observing you.

But remember, we don't have to be trapped by destructive, negative communication patterns. Through the empowering of God's Spirit we really can form new, liberating feelings, attitudes and actions that communicate to our children a joyful, loving way of life.

● ● ●

FOR REFLECTION, DISCUSSION
AND ACTION

*1. Make a conscious effort to monitor what you say to your kids this week. (Enlist your wife to help you.) Is the majority of your communication with them negative or positive? Write down two specific ways you are going to try to make interactions with your children more positive and affirming.

2. When was the last time you can remember really listening to what your kids had to say? Can they come to you freely, knowing that you're "all ears" when they talk? What one change will you make, beginning immediately, in your listening skills to improve your communication with your children?

3. Make a date with each one of your children this week. Set aside at least one hour with each child and do something he or she wants to do.

*4. What specific ideas came to mind as you read this chapter that can help enhance the communication you have with your children? List at least five ideas that you would like to put into practice. Then develop an "action plan." What specifically are you going to do to put your ideas to work?

Saying "You Are Special!"

(Norm)

*K*ids want to be hugged and told they're special.

During a recent stay in Phoenix, Josh received so many invitations to speak to high school assemblies that several of the gatherings had to be held outside during noontime. At one school he stood on a large rock to speak to the overflow crowd. Just as he began, a group of punk rockers, sporting yards of chains and fluorescent hair, walked up to within twenty feet of where he stood.

As soon as Josh finished his talk and stepped down from the rock, the punk leader ran up to him. The entire crowd gasped. What the 1,000 or so students didn't see or hear was the punk rocker, with tears streaming down his cheeks, asking Josh to hug him. As Josh said "Yes," the kid grabbed him, put his head on Josh's shoulder and cried.

The hug lasted about a minute—a long hug for a punk rocker! Finally, he let go of Josh and through his tears he explained, "My father has never hugged me or ever said 'I love you.'"

This young man was crying out for the love, intimacy and attention of his father. His clothes and physical appearance were not a sign of rebellion, but rather a crying out for attention and love . . . the love and attention of his *father*.

Several months ago Winnie and I invited Debbie (not her real name) a young, unmarried, pregnant woman to live with us for a few weeks until a permanent home became available. Eventually she moved in with Gene and Carolyn Johnson, a dedicated couple who have a significant ministry to unmarried, pregnant women.

Recently the Johnsons were visiting in our home and they mentioned their desire to write a book about their experiences with unmarried mothers-to-be. Turning to his wife, Gene said, "Tell them what we would title the book." Carolyn replied, "We'd call it *I Just Want to Be Held*. The majority of the girls who have come through our home have said this to us at some time."

In their longing to be cherished and treated as somebody special, those young women turned to a romantic relationship and fell prey to sexual involvement that resulted in pregnancy. Yet these romantic relationships only temporarily met their need. When the relationships were over, the young women were left with an infant and a bleak future.

Meeting the Real Need

Often conscious or unconscious sexual expressions indicate a deeper need in a person — a need that he is trying to meet through sexual acts. *Sexual expressions often manifest the deeper, more basic human needs encompassing our personhood.*

The act of masturbation is an example. When is a person more likely to practice masturbation? When he is lonely. When he has been rejected. When he is bored. When he wants to be loved. Such a person tries to meet these basic fulfillment needs through self-manipulation. The problem with wrong sexual behaviors is that they never really meet the basic need. Instead, they create a vicious cycle: temporary release, which often leads to guilt feelings, which cause increased longing and eventually a drive for satisfaction, which results in temporary release, etc.

Because sexuality is rooted in our psyche, premarital or extra-marital sexual involvement often indicates an inadequate way of coping with a problem—a sign that a basic need is not being met through the channels God designed. This truth should challenge us as dads, for whenever we nurture our children's basic needs, as God intended, we are protecting them from sexual exploitation. The more healthy a child's total personality is, the less vulnerable he will be to his own physical desires and to manipulation by others. If we want our sons and daughters to have strength to withstand the sexual pressure, we must focus our attention on the very basic root issues.

Your child has a deep-seated need to be significant. God intends for this normal, healthy need to be met first by you and your child's mother. Before the youngster can comprehend the concept of "God," he is being shaped by his human parents. Before he knows there is a God, and can find significance in Him, his parents must fill that void. If Mom and Dad do not satisfy this hunger and point the child to his heavenly Father, he wanders through life seeking someone or something to fill this emotional void. If left unmet, this drive will lead to behaviors that can destroy the child—or seriously cripple his life.

Kids Are Special!

Before we explore ways to nurture our children's need for significance, let's look at four reasons they really are "special."

First, *our children are special because they have*

been created in the image of God. What is that image? God is both infinite and personal. We are like Him in His personhood. That involves the ability to relate, to create and to make moral choices. It involves the emotions, the intellect and the soul. It's true that sin has marred and dimmed that image. Nevertheless, we all are special because we each reflect some of God's likeness. We possess an inner nature, an inner life that is somehow akin to who God is.

Jesus recognized the significance of all people. He was sensitive to the downtrodden, the diseased and the children because He knew they were especially vulnerable to being looked down on as common or undesirable. He sought them out, lifted them up, treated them with special consideration and communicated His love to them. Second, *our children are special because they are fellow members or potential members of God's eternal family.* This truth takes on a special meaning when we realize that our *eternal* relationship with our children is as a brother, not a father. This new perspective should increase our respect and consideration of them, and destroy the tendency to look down on them. Each family member has honor as a member of God's family, no matter what their age.

Third, *children are special because they enrich our lives.* Psalm 127:3 says that children are a special gift from a loving heavenly Father. When our children are born we accept this by faith. We believe that the Lord gave us this family member to add some special ingredient to our family and to our lives personally.

Acknowledging that children enrich our lives is not a lofty, abstract truth. God uses children as one of the primary ingredients to motivate us to growth. They, more than anyone else, can challenge us to become the person we can be through God's grace. Children help us discover God's perspective on relationships. As we grasp how we feel toward our children, we can better appreciate how our Father feels about us.

One of my daughters has learning disabilities. She is classified by the school system as mentally handicapped and grouped with other students in a self-contained classroom. Our society has difficulty treating these individuals with equal dignity and honor.

As a Christian father, however, I have discovered and thanked God for her incomparable significance to me and my family. Her contribution to our family is equal to that of every other member. By believing in my daughter's unique place in our family, we have communicated respect and honor to her in such a way that her personality is released to thrive and express her giftedness. She is genuinely significant.

Fourth, *our children are special because of their uniqueness, personality, talents and giftedness.* Accept this as a given at your child's birth. Anticipate that he will be different from you, his mother, his brothers and sisters, and prize that rather than criticize it.

Many children today do not experience the family spirit that celebrates the uniqueness of its members. Harold Smith, in an article titled "Superkids and Superparents," observes that

> Rather than viewing children as complex and uniquely individual personalities to be molded over time, we are increasingly, to use Dr. Bruno Bettelheim's words, "equating child-rearing to mass-producing machinery"; and we are basing the "quality of production" on standardized criteria — all to the exclusion of the child's own emotional and spiritual dynamics."[1]

Listen, by contrast, to Dawn as she tells of her family experience in which she received respect and value from her mother and father:

> When I first began to think about what [my

parents] did right, their appreciation for us as individuals with different gifts stood out most in my
mind.

My sister and I did well academically, enjoying things like memorizing and writing essays. Our
two brothers were into writing, acting, art, poetry.
They enjoyed creating. All of us were encouraged to
learn, to develop good study habits, to do well in
school. At the same time, we felt great freedom and
lack of pressure because of our parents' refusal to
place value judgments on our abilities. [My parents]
were study-oriented, for example, yet they accepted
the boys' creative gifts with as much praise and encouragement as any academic achievement.[2]

Every child needs an affirmation of his own uniqueness. This feeling of personal significance enables a
child to use his mental and emotional resources for the
constructive development of his life. The child who lacks
this sense of personal importance and value diverts energy to fill this bottomless pit and finds it difficult to
prosper emotionally. As a father, one of your primary
ministries to your children is that of nurturing their
sense of personal significance — the "I'm special" feeling
that promotes healthy development. We now turn to
that task.

Nurturing the "I'm Special" Feeling

Remember Debbie, the pregnant young lady
mentioned at the beginning of this chapter? We've met
many "Debbies" in our years of counseling people. Talking to them prompts a feeling of sadness. They are
women who have a constant hunger to be affirmed,
hugged, cherished. Somewhere along the way, their
fathers neglected this vital function and produced
children starving for emotional nourishment.

One of the most basic ways to meet a child's need
for significance is to *cherish* him. You cherish your child

when you are physically affectionate with a hug or kiss, when you speak fondly to him, when you look lovingly at him. Cherishing begins with an underlying attitude of delight you have toward your wife and children. This attitude says in words and actions, "I like you; I think you're special; I'm delighted that God sent you into my life." *A child who sees his mother cherished, and who is himself cherished, will thrive.*

In his book *The Total Man,* Dan Benson reflects on the value of these moments in his childhood:

> I'll never forget the Family Hugs that often took place in our kitchen as I was growing up. Toddling through the doorway, I'd see Dad wrapping Mom in his arms (not an unusual sight in our home). That made me feel good inside. So good that I couldn't resist joining them ... So I'd charge across the kitchen linoleum and wrap my arms around their legs. Mom and Dad were always happy to include me. If any other brothers were around, they would sometimes join in as the family hug got bigger and bigger.
>
> Mom and Dad made our house a loving home, more by example than by lecture. We were secure as children because Dad took the lead in making the home atmosphere one of love and joy.[3]

Cherishing is not the same as accepting. To accept is an expression of unconditional love, *agape* love. It says, "I accept you as you are, for God created you in His image." It says, "You are of great value and have personal dignity totally apart from what you do."

Your child can exist with acceptance only, but to prosper he must be cherished. Cherishing is like an essential nutrient a plant must receive if it is to become strong, healthy and mature. A gardener would be foolish to withhold fertilizer and produce a stunted, unproductive plant. Why, then, do we withhold what will enrich our children the most and build the greatest strength and fruitfulness in their lives?

You may find it hard to cherish your child—to be physically affectionate with your son or daughter. You may have received little or none from your own father. Josh and I didn't when we were kids. But someone has to break the cycle: *We can begin to take small steps of warm, tender actions that grow over time.*

The time to begin is when your child is born; that way the act of cherishing becomes integrated into your relationship at the initial bonding stage and continues throughout his lifetime. When your daughter is a toddler, she naturally crawls up into your lap and enjoys your arms around her. When she is an adolescent, she still needs to be able to come to Dad when she is lonely, discouraged or just hungry for a hug and find the same warm, affectionate father there to nurture her. The daughter who receives this feels cherished by her dad and will not need to go outside the home to be affirmed and cherished by another man, one who might take advantage of her sexually.

Dad, though both sons and daughters need to receive your affection, we believe it is especially vital that you not withhold it from your daughter. You may be apt to avoid physical contact with your daughter because she is a woman. Many men find it difficult to hug and cuddle their adolescent daughters. You may hold back when it's obvious she needs the security of physical comfort and love. Avoid this tendency. You, above everyone else, are the one by whom she will measure her worth.

Not long ago Josh spoke at Fishnet, a large outdoor music festival and teaching conference held on a farm in Virginia. That morning while speaking on "Why Wait?" he told the young people in the crowd of about 12,000 that they were special and to never forget that they were worth waiting for.

Later that morning Josh noticed a young blonde girl, about twelve years old, following him. He stopped and asked, "Did you want to see me?"

She replied rather shyly, "Do you really think I'm special?"

"Yes! God made you special and don't you ever forget it." Josh cautiously put his arms around her shoulders and gave her a tender hug as a father would his daughter. She burst into tears and said, "You don't know how long I've waited for that. My mom and dad divorced five years ago, and my dad has never hugged me or told me I'm special."

Five days later as Josh left for the airport, a note was slipped to him by a security man who said a little girl wanted him to have it. The tightly folded note had just six words written in red:

Thank you for loving me . . . Koreen.

Girls like Koreen are vulnerable to the first guy who says, "I want to show my love to you!" If a child does not find that love and intimacy in her father, it becomes almost impossible to turn it down from another male.

You can cherish your child in non-physical ways as well. Writing a note that tells your child what you admire about him will communicate your affection. Don't be afraid to use warm words that express tenderness, gentleness, caring and prizing. Or, cherish your child by spoken words as you go for a walk, ride together in the car or as you put the child to bed. These words express your delight with the child, your awareness of his specialness and your admiration of certain personality strengths.

When these are accompanied by smiles, hugs and other expressions of affection, they build a reservoir from which your child draws refreshment throughout his life.

Other Ways to Show You Care

Beyond cherishing, there are other ways you can communicate a sense of significance to your child. For example, you can *model your own sense of being special to God*. In your conversations with family members you will inevitably reveal how you think God feels about you. In an earlier chapter we encouraged you to be open and transparent with your children. This is an important place to practice that.

Children can hear "You're special!" in husband-wife conversations. When a child hears and sees Dad cherish Mom, cherishing is modeled in another way before the child. Mentioning to your children ways your spouse enriches your life, and how you admire her personality, talents and gifts displays to the child your thoughts and feelings about others.

In essence the family is the environment in which children receive the blessing of affirmation. Lance Craw, who is married and has two young daughters, was deeply affected after reading *The Blessing* by Gary Smalley and John Trent. In this timely book the authors describe how our heavenly Father is a God of blessing—it is inherent in His nature. Then, they proceed to demonstrate how vital it is that we be communicators of these blessings, especially to family members.

Lance determined to take the idea of blessing seriously and began a regular event at the evening meal. He would place his hands on his wife Holly and pray a blessing on her. Then he would move to each child and pray a blessing on them. The children expressed delight with this and soon wanted to participate in blessing family members. As Lance related the enthusiastic response of his children, you could see what a joy it was to him. Having discovered and applied the principle in one setting, he is now sensitive to other places where he can continue to encourage this enriching experience.

As we cherish our children while they are growing up, they will recall precious memories of words we've said and hugs we've shared in the years to come. Even more valuable than that are the warm, positive feelings our children will have of being valued as a special person by their father.

• • •

FOR REFLECTION, DISCUSSION AND ACTION

1. Reflect on the statement, "Your child has a deep-seated need to be significant." What does the word *significant* mean to you? What do you think it means to your wife, and to each of your children?

*2. Why are your children special in God's sight? Think of each child by name, and list at least five specific reasons why each one is special to Him, and to you. What are you doing to let each one know how significant he is?

3. After reviewing the latter part of this chapter, define the word *cherish* in your own words. In what specific ways are you cherishing each of your children? What can you begin doing to cherish them even more?

*4. Give each of your kids at least one warm hug and at least one genuine "I love you and I'm proud of you" this week. Then make it a regular practice!

Building Your Child's Self-Esteem
(Josh)

*H*ave you ever wondered what hereditary or environ-
mental factors determine the difference between a
responsible, trustworthy young adult and a weak, susceptible one?

Norm and I believe one of the key factors is the
degree and quality of esteem those young adults hold for
themselves. And as we are about to see, dads have always
played an important role in helping determine the
quality of self-esteem that develops in their children.

Dad Made a Difference

Joseph, son of Jacob, was an intriguing young
man. He encountered a series of hardships that would
devastate many men, but he moved through them with
perseverance and dignity. No matter what situation he
was in, he manifested a distinct sense of God's presence
and care.

In Genesis 37, we are told that Joseph enjoyed a
meaningful relationship with his father. Joseph's birth

touched a tender spot in his father's heart. Jacob had a special love for Rachel, the infant's mother. This child was the fulfillment of a mother's prayer and a father's yearning. Joseph was the recipient of his father's unconditional love and attentiveness.

Thus, from his earliest years, Joseph knew the security of a strong father-son relationship.

Throughout his life, Joseph had an unusually strong sense of God's love and presence, very likely due to the deep love he sensed from his earthly father. This sustained him in times of intense trial. Joseph also handled pressure, injustice and disappointment very effectively. He was able to avoid sexual temptation, even though his stand led to imprisonment. His father's nurturing love had established strong emotional resources that could sustain him in times of loneliness and hurt.

In today's jargon we'd say that Jacob played a major role in building Joseph's self-esteem. Joseph eventually weathered the storms he encountered to become a godly man used to deliver his own family and the entire Egyptian nation from disaster. The Lord was obviously working in Joseph's life, yet we can also see that He used a loving father to prepare a son for the task set before him.

The way a person perceives himself powerfully shapes his attitudes, feelings, behavior and actions. Dr. Paul Meier of the Minirth-Meier Clinic makes this pointed observation: "Two of the most important concepts I learned from my psychiatric training, both of which agree totally with Scripture, are: *(1) You cannot truly love others until you learn to love yourself in a healthy way; and (2) Lack of self-worth is the basis of most psychological problems.*"[1]

Our self-image establishes the perimeters of our life, and we cannot see ourselves going beyond those limits. We may *wish* we could, but we don't believe that it is possible. Joseph became the powerful, godly leader he was largely due to his father's positive influence on his self-esteem.

Strength to Stand Strong

Unfortunately, our self-esteem is tugged at by forces other than the family. Mom and Dad have the first and greatest opportunity to help mold our self-esteem, but other powerful agents are at work to manipulate our minds. The 20th century has unleashed a vast host of impersonal cultural messengers that incessantly convince us of what we should think and be.

We are told that we must perform to be worthwhile. Those with the looks, abilities and brains win the prizes. Our educational system rewards the intelligent and subtly degrades those not endowed with high IQs. Who receives the majority of college scholarships? Those who are the *best and the brightest* — the most intelligent, the greatest athletes, or the most attractive. Those who have not been endowed with physical, mental or social skills soon learn that they are the losers.

Media messages subtly shape our thinking about what is acceptable and what is not acceptable. And it's not hard to see that media standards of right and wrong are rarely in agreement with God's standards. Television shows, movies, music and magazines tell our children what is popular sexual behavior. One teenager notes how the message comes across to him:

> I want to keep sexually pure but everywhere I turn I'm told to "make out," to jump into bed. It's the subject of my friends, I see it on the tube. I hear it in the music. It seems like everybody's saying, "Don't miss out. Get your share."

Society uses emotional manipulation to pressure

us to conform. People who are not in with the latest fashion, not living in the fast lane, not having erotic sexual encounters are made to feel inferior. In many ways our children and youth feel that pressure more keenly than we do. They face greater peer pressure, they are more music and entertainment conscious, and they face more pressure to look good physically, mentally and socially.

Despite these pressures, there is hope. Think back on Joseph for a moment. He was rudely ripped from his father's care and deposited into an alien, hostile, ungodly environment. Despite all that, Joseph voluntarily chose to live consistent with the values and spiritual realities he had been taught!

Joseph's story demonstrates that it is possible for our children to gain a strong self-image that can empower them to stand strong in an immoral society.

What Your Child Needs

If you analyze what most experts say about healthy self-esteem you will notice three basic concepts. If you know how to implement these in your parenting, you are well on the road to success. You will inevitably face special problems and concerns, but if you keep working on the basics, your child will prosper in the long haul.

A Sense of Belonging

To begin with, *self-esteem thrives where the child gains a sense of belonging.* When a child looks forward to coming home because it is a warm and secure place, his need for security and safety is being met. The home setting that welcomes the child as he comes through the doors will always be a haven, a place of retreat.

Many children come home from school to an empty house. Whatever problems or conflicts they have faced will have to wait for Mom and Dad's arrival from work. Too often the parents come home tired and want nothing more than to read the paper or watch TV, when in fact their day is not done until they have taken the time to joyfully interact or play with their children.

It is a fact of our culture that if our children don't feel they belong at home, they will look elsewhere. As we have seen, young people will often combat feelings of loneliness with sexual encounters. Sue, a high school junior, expressed it well: "I felt so alone. Mom and Dad were always too busy to have time for me. When Ted befriended me I was ecstatic. He listened to me. He would hold me and console me. He really seemed to care about me."

What most teens find is that sexual activity pursued to fill the void of loneliness becomes addictive. As Holly talked about her sexual involvement she, too, came to see that she was trying to fill a deeper void. She said, "After I'd been touched like that I needed it again and again. The more I felt loved the more I was driven to repeat it."

Let's put this in a positive light. Dad, you have a unique capacity to make your children feel that they belong, that someone cares about them, that they are an important part of your life. Having this emotional haven in you gives them strength to withstand sexual pressures. Your love and friendship with them says, "I cherish (esteem) you," and gives them a basis by which to esteem themselves.

A Need for Personal Worth

The second concept basic to self-esteem is this: *Your child needs a sense of personal worth.* The issues in Chapter 8 reflect this principle. Somehow a person must gain the belief and feeling that he is a person of value. Both Norm and I are convinced that parents are primarily responsible for developing their children's self-worth, and that the task is incomplete if Dad doesn't do his part.

One Sunday I was invited to speak to the San Diego Chargers in their pre-game chapel. I took my son Sean, and after chapel we found our seats in the stadium. The team had given us seats down front, near the 50-yard line! Fifty thousand spectators filled the stadium and the roar was deafening.

I put one arm around my son and said, "Look at all these people, Buddy." Sean turned 360 degrees in his seat to see everyone, especially those way up high. To those ten-year-old eyes it looked like the whole world was there.

"Wow, Dad," Sean exclaimed, "that's a lot of people!"

"Yes, it is. But you know what? You mean more to me than all these people put together. Son, what you think of me as your dad means more to me than the opinion of all fifty thousand people!"

Sean's eyes grew big. Again he surveyed the entire stadium. Then, with his childish excitement, he exclaimed: "Really, Dad? More than all them?" He jumped on my lap, feeling very secure and significant. At that moment, Sean knew he counted.

We encourage you to look for those natural opportunities to make each of your children feel the same way. But first you must really believe that your children count. You must have a settled conviction that your children are precious . . . of eternal value to you and to God. Your certainty will then come through loud and clear in your words, mannerisms and behavior toward them.

Norm often asks parents during counseling sessions, "Do you frequently put your arms around your child, look into his eyes with delight and say, 'I'm glad the Lord sent you into my life. You are one of His wonderful gifts to me'?" Sadly, Norm has discovered that many parents have *never* done that. They cannot remember a time when they expressed their joy over the child's presence in their family. Yet, the child who receives such wholehearted affirmation is ten times more likely to flourish.

We can monitor our attitude toward our children by our approach to discipline. One dad disciplines by criticizing or condemning his child. He is sensitive to every mistake, pounces on him and makes sure the child feels ashamed. Another dad views the same situation in a different light. He recognizes that a mistake has been made, but treats the child as though he is worthy of respect. He sits down and in a thoughtful, kind manner helps the child think through what went wrong. He helps his child see the consequences of his action and guides him in corrective steps. The process is not degrading or shameful. This dad is also quick to see the positive qualities in his child's life and more often compliments him on his strengths than berating his weaknesses. By focusing on the child's virtues, he motivates him toward excelling in his strengths rather than dwelling on failures.

A Sense of Competence

There is yet a third concept basic to self-esteem: *Your child needs a growing sense of competence.* All children have a natural desire to do well. As parents we can encourage our children in their attempts and congratulate them on their accomplishments. Unfortunately, there are several reasons why a child may not achieve his sense of competence easily.

Adults tend to measure a child's ability by adult standards (at times we can be rather mindless creatures). Check out yourself. Do you expect your child to function at your adult level of competence? Do you expect your daughter to wash the car as well as you wash it? Do you expect your son to make his bed as neatly as you do? How much consideration is given to their limited knowledge and lack of coordination? Most adults even talk to children using adult words, rather than using words easily understood by children.

Many parents expect their children to be competent without training. How many skills are involved in making a bed, washing a car and mowing the lawn? Yet, most parents assign tasks without giving adequate guidance: "You're old enough to clean your own room now. Do it! And do it right!"

When we do give our children guidance on a task, we also need to give them the freedom to fail. Should they fail, we need to encourage them to complete the task instead of belittling them and their efforts. *Praise* what has been accomplished and *motivate* your child to finish the task left undone: "The outside of the car looks great! You did a nice job. But the inside needs some sprucing up. How about vacuuming the inside?"

There are influences outside your family which affect your child's sense of competence as well. We live in a competitive society. We constantly find ourselves pitted against others and their abilities on the job, at school, on the athletic field. Unfortunately there is always someone who does things just a little better than we do. Many of us are far down the ladder of competence in some areas of our lives, so when we are consistently measured against superior performers, our self-confidence is easily eroded.

Nourishing a sense of competence in our children is a long-term event that requires much thought and planning. It also requires that we actively involve ourselves in our children's lives as *positive guides* who are slow to find fault and quick to affirm new levels of growth. We need to help them embrace a true assessment of their strengths and accept their limitations without self-condemnation.

A father has the opportunity to create a positive environment in the home — one that draws out his children's strengths, nurtures and reinforces them, and instills within his children a sense of delight about who they are.

Self-esteem and Sexual Wholeness

There is direct interplay between a father, his child's self-esteem and his child's sexual attitudes. We have seen how our children daily confront a sexually distorted, sexually confused and sexually intense society. For them to cope with it on their own is disastrous. Our kids are too immature and vulnerable to stand against the determination and sophistication of an ungodly culture. Our children need to develop inner strength, bred into them through loving, nurturing parents. Otherwise, they will become pawns at the mercy of those who would exploit them.

The evidence indicates that children who have *both* parents working together to nourish a healthy self-esteem will be far more likely to develop healthy sexual attitudes and behavior patterns. A child with positive self-esteem can more easily say "No!" to his own sexual desires and to pressure from someone dedicated to seducing him. And you, Dad, play a crucial role in building your child's healthy personal identity. Armand Nicholi states it well:

> If one factor influences the character development and emotional stability of a person, it is the quality of the relationship he experiences as a child with both of his parents. Conversely, if people suffering from severe non-organic emotional illness have one experience in common, it is the absence of a parent through death, divorce, a time-demanding job or ab-

sence for other reasons. A parent's inaccessibility either physically, emotionally, or both, can exert a profound influence on the child's emotional health.[2]

These thoughts are encouraging because they tell us we *can* have a powerful influence on our sons and daughters. We can equip our kids with the emotional and spiritual resources that will allow them to cope far more effectively with the pressures they're facing. And they will be far less likely to be driven by powerful, destructive inner needs or exploited by a misguided, but determined, society.

What a privilege we have as dads — to be able to make a difference in our children's lives!

● ● ●

FOR REFLECTION, DISCUSSION AND ACTION

1. What is the difference between a positive self-image and an inflated ego? How do you know?

2. Take a moment and evaluate the self-esteem of each of your children. Do they seem happy with who they are? Have you noticed any behavior which may indicate they have a poor self-image?

*3. What specific factors are at work in your children's lives right now that could detract from a healthy self-image? What, specifically, can you be doing as their dad to help them through these pressures?

*4. Think of two things you can do for each of your children this week that will let them know how valuable they are to you and to society. When and how will you implement these ideas?

Nurturing
Christian Values
(Norm)

Whether we realize it or not, our kids are looking to us for the values that will guide their future decisions.

Sixteen-year-old Carl wrote to us of the influence his parents had on his sexual attitudes and behavior: "At school the air is heavy with talk about 'making out.' Sex among the guys is the big conquest. It's like, 'How many notches do ya' have on your belt?'

"But Mom and Dad have really helped me see that sex is different from what the guys say. They have emphasized that girls are special in a different way. They are my 'spiritual sisters,' not somebody to make out with or someone to satisfy my sexual desires. At times it's tough because I hear so much that says otherwise, but I really do believe God's way is the right way."

One challenge we face as parents is to instill in our children a deep and abiding respect for those with whom they relate. It's our job to nourish a strong sense of sacredness about another person's sexuality so that our sons do not infringe upon what is not rightfully theirs and our daughters do not yield to those who want to exploit them. These beliefs come from a biblically based value system. The key is imparting these values to our children in such a way that they embrace them as their own.

How do we do it?

First we must confirm that our home environment encourages the growth of responsible, Christlike values. Is your home warm, secure and accepting? Or cold, unstable and demanding?

Jerry has come to talk with me several times. He has many unhealthy habits that plague him, yet his parents' attitudes have done little to help him overcome his problems. "I feel guilty much of the time because my mom is constantly criticizing me. 'When are you going to quit smoking?' she says again and again. The way she says it makes me feel small and dirty. I feel like running away and hiding."

Jerry has lived with condemning parents for so long that he believes God regards him the same way. He sees the Bible's value system as nothing but a bunch of straitlaced rules designed to tie him down, make him feel guilty and complicate his life. If Jerry's parents were more supportive and compassionate, truer models of the *agape* love of Jesus Christ, he would be better able to discover Christ's liberating power and more likely to adopt Christian values as his own.

Within the environment of a warm, supportive, nurturing home, we can plant and grow strong spiritual values. Let's investigate three ways we can make this happen.

Actions Speak Louder...

Values are communicated, first, *by example.* In Deuteronomy 6:1-9 the Lord tells the children of Israel how they are to lead their children to godliness and purity. He emphasizes that the parents themselves must love Him sincerely and follow His commands. In verse 6 He says, "These commandments that I give you today are to be upon your *hearts*" (italics added). If children are to experientially grasp how one loves God, they must see it lived out in their parents' daily lives.

Are you setting the example for your children's lives? Fellow dads, without even realizing it, too many of us have virtually defaulted in this area. We may be short-tempered but expect our children to be angelic; we may be enslaved to a habit such as overeating or too much TV, while preaching the evils of other harmful practices. We may model anxiety and lack of trust in practical matters, while wanting our children to embrace the sovereignty of God.

We know of one dad who is usually morose and inaccessible around his family, yet when he pulls the station wagon into the church parking lot on Sunday mornings, he's suddenly all smiles. Now he wonders why his oldest son regards Christians as hypocrites.

Jesus reaffirmed the importance of positive role modeling. In Luke 6:40 He said, "A student is not above his teacher, but everyone who is fully trained will be like his teacher." Notice He didn't say that the student would know what the teacher knows. He said that the student will become *like* the teacher. A close association and mutual respect between teacher and student results in the student's thinking process and actions bearing a likeness to the teacher's. Likewise, if we maintain an intimate, loving relationship with our children, they will bear our likeness and probably will not diverge from our value system for any lengthy period of time.

God has designed a powerful imaging process between parent and child. The child is imprinted with the parent's likeness because of the bonding that occurs on a day-to-day basis. If you, Dad, are the strong orbit around which your child revolves, he will absorb your likeness, your values and your view of life. Plenty of research supports this truth: Values are formed through *relationships*. The stronger the relationship, the greater the value formation.

Jean, a mature, radiant Christian woman, wrote us that her father was the most influential person in her life. "I write this of [my dad] because it was his character and example that were the strongest influence on my life, though he enforced them also with precepts . . . His faults were the faults of his virtues, as the French say, and though he has now been dead for fifty years, I often find myself thinking how pleased he would be with this or that."[1]

Think of that! A dad's legacy enduring for fifty years!

Dennis Rainey, in his book *Pulling Weeds, Planting Seeds,* has devoted two full chapters as tributes to his mother and father. Of this father, Rainey writes:

> As an impressionable young boy, my radar caught more of [Dad's] life than he ever knew. During my perilous teenage years he was the model and hero I needed—and he still is. He taught me the importance of hard work and completing a task. I learned about lasting commitment from him—I never feared my parents would divorce. My dad was absolutely committed to my mom. I felt secure and protected.
>
> Most importantly, he taught me about *character.* He did what was right, even when no one was looking. I never heard him talk about cheating on taxes—he paid them and didn't grumble. His integrity was impeccable. I never heard him lie, and his eyes always demanded the same truth in return. The mental image of his character still fuels and energizes my life today.[2]

Would your kids be able to write such a tribute of you someday?

We suggest that you spend time evaluating what your child is absorbing day to day through your actions. The following questions may be helpful in this process:

    1. What do my actions tell my children about what it means to be a man?

    2. What do my actions toward my wife tell my children about what it means to respect and cherish a member of the opposite sex?

    3. How are my attitudes and behaviors serving as a model of the Lord's attitudes and behaviors toward my son or daughter?

...But Words Are Important, Too

A second way values are communicated to our children is *through our words.* All of us have indelible impressions of things our fathers stressed over and over through our childhood and teen years. Or we may recall some significant event in which they spoke of a conviction with such intensity that its message left a permanent mark on us.

Solomon emphasized the value and power of words when he appealed to kids to pay close attention to their parents' admonishments: "My son, observe the commandment of your father, and do not forsake the teaching of your mother" (Proverbs 6:20).

In verbalizing values we need to be cautious about relying on negative communication. Moralizing, criticizing, arguing and commanding are not very effective approaches. We need to use restraint when tempted to relate to our children with a list of rules and regulations. Occasionally our children need to feel our wrath at their persistent disobedience, but those times should be infrequent and balanced with abundant words that note our children's strengths and positive qualities. In addition, these confrontive times should come after genuine prayer for guidance and direction from the Holy Spirit; they should not be prompted by our own impatience.

The words that will best shape our child's values are those that are positive, given to reinforce some positive behavior or attitude the child has demonstrated. *Our children are not strengthened when we point out what they've done wrong, but when we commend them for what they've done right.* This principle can motivate us to use positive words, words that strengthen and reinforce our children's wise choices and actions.

You can also use words to be transparent with your children. I remember when my son Joel was going through a hard time as a result of an unwise choice he had made. One day we went for a walk together, and Joel unloaded his woes on me.

As we walked I shared an incident from my own teen years. I, too, had faced a similar situation, responded unwisely, and experienced the consequences of that decision.

By sharing my own story, I think Joel saw that though I did not condone his actions, I wasn't standing in ivory-towered judgment. He saw that I wanted to be his teammate, not his judge. This encouraged him to open up further and allowed me to help him in thinking through his situation.

Our children may use us as sounding boards to test ideas or values that we may not espouse. Perhaps a healthy perspective in these situations is that we consider it an honor that our children would trust our opinion enough to come to us for help. If we are committed to positive communication, we will not attack or criticize our children's thoughts, but demonstrate respect and courtesy even as we investigate and evaluate the ideas they have shared.

Some dads get inflamed if their children express a view not in harmony with their own; yet our children need a safe environment in which to express their thoughts and test ideas. If they find us unwilling to listen and understand, they'll soon stop sharing their concerns with us altogether. Our openness will keep the communication channel clear for dialogue about differences as well as similarities.

One last thought about communicating values through words: *Express your own convictions.* This is another arena where fathers tend to lose by default. Our children hear others express what they cherish, desire and feel strongly about, but never hear their own dad express his convictions and goals. Verbalize those truths that you cherish with conviction, yet with kindness and graciousness. Let your child know that you believe in sexual purity. Let your child know that it is biblically correct—and therefore wise—to not get sexually involved before marriage. Let your child know that you deeply respect women and believe that men should treat them with dignity and honor.

What you don't tell your child *can* hurt him.

Help Them Internalize Biblical Values

The third way we nurture values is by helping our children *internalize* them. Our children may see godly values in our lives and may hear us speak with conviction, but unless they internalize their beliefs through careful thought and decision, they will be vulnerable to erosion by outside forces. James 1:22-24 suggests that we might hear truth, but not be led to apply it in day-to-day situations.

Our children may have the right answers, but the wrong attitudes. Our goal is to nurture *internal motivation* that will drive our children to honor Jesus Christ, live responsible, productive, others-centered lives that flow out of a relationship with Him, and practice obedience as a consequence of the love relationship with Him (John 14:21-24).

Internalizing values is a process. First we need *information* or truth to work with. Then, through interaction with another, we *test* the facts to see if they are valid and how they apply. This is where you, Dad, can be vitally involved — graciously, thoughtfully, eagerly talking with your child. Question him and encourage him to question. Seek out new insights, new facts, new truth. You do not do this *for* your child, but *with* him, leading him to form his convictions on solid foundations.

After information-seeking and testing, the process will lead to the third step: *building* this conviction into our children's lifestyle. Here biblical principles become daily experience. Through practicing what we preach, our children discover that biblical values lead to fruitful, meaningful living.

In essence the internalizing process involves: (1) making choices freely from alternatives as a result of carefully considering the facts and consequences; (2) embracing the choice in the sense of being willing to publicly espouse it; and (3) acting on the choice in some tangible way. The value choice becomes a part of our lifestyle, integrated into daily decisions and actions.

The process of internalization is lifelong. The formation of one's own values does not begin until the early teenage years. Younger children simply do not have the mental maturity to process abstract ideas. During the earlier years parents model and teach values, and children stockpile resources for future use. As our children move into the teenage phase, we then emphasize those actions that help them internalize and personalize the issues they are encountering.

There is one more important principle about internalization we'd like to share with you: Our children's

value system does not have to be an exact duplicate of
our value system. We are not in the business of making
clones of ourselves. Each child is a unique and separate
person. They may have different ideas on certain subjects, feel more strongly on other issues, and perhaps just
plain disagree with us at times — and still be following
biblical guidelines in the values they adhere to. If their
relationship with the Lord is solid, and if they are not
going against a clear biblical standard, allow them the
freedom to think differently from you. Happy is the child
whose parents also respect *his* values — or at least his
right to have them.

Nurturing a strong value system is not easy. But
as you have seen, there are many ways to help your child
grow toward internalizing responsible values. But we've
yet to mention the greatest way to impact your child's
value system: Introduce him to a genuine relationship
with Jesus Christ. Out of that walk with Christ comes a
way of life that embraces a fully Christlike lifestyle.

● ● ●

FOR REFLECTION, DISCUSSION AND ACTION

1. How have your recent actions been communicating values
to your children? Do you see any adjustments that need to be
made?

2. When was the last time you verbalized to your children a
conviction you hold? Describe their response. If you could do
it again, what would you do or say differently? Is there something you can share with them this week that will assist them
in their value formation process?

*3. If you were to write a paragraph about each of your
children's value systems, what would you say? Do you have
enough information to make a fair evaluation? Are you encouraged by what you see developing?

*4. Why not try the exercise above? Go over what you've written with your wife to get her insight as well. Then discuss what you need to do from this point forward to continue nurturing a Christian value system in each of your children.

Helping Your Child Handle Peer Pressure

(Josh)

*C*onsider thirteen-year-old Marie's predicament. Her school sponsored an eighth grade graduation dance, and a boy in her class invited Marie to go with him.

She accepted the date. When her parents found out, they were irate.

"Your mom and I don't want you to date until you're sixteen," her dad said.

Marie was flabbergasted. "No one in my school thinks that way today, Dad," she lamented. "I'd be *so* embarrassed to tell my girlfriends that my parents think I'm too young to date. They'd laugh at me and rub it in my face!"

From the beginning of history man has faced psychological pressure to conform to someone else's ideas of how to live. Peer pressure is that subtle force that coerces us into complying with what our associates say is acceptable. It creeps into our thoughts and feelings, raising questions of whether others will like us if we do not fit in with *their* patterns, activities and values.

We face peer pressure. Our parents faced peer pressure, and their parents before that. But what is unique about today's adolescent peer pressure is its unprecedented pull. Never before has there been such an overpowering youth subculture that so masterfully attracts, convinces and shapes the thoughts, desires and behavior of a vast segment of today's young people. A majority of the music, television programs, movies and clothing is targeted toward these powerful (and bankable) youth. In past generations young people copied the standards and actions of adults; today adults often follow the trends and lifestyles of youth.

Neutralizing Unhealthy Peer Pressure

Youth, more than anyone else, are especially vulnerable to peer pressure. They are at that tender psychological state in which they are endeavoring to establish their identity, and so are more emotionally and socially insecure. If their past history has been littered with failure, rejection and insecurity, they will be even more susceptible to the influences of their friends as they long for acceptance and that overpowering desire to "belong."

Our children cannot avoid peer pressure. Some of that pressure will reflect passing fads that are just a part of growing up. Other influences will be unhealthy coercion that can erode values or establish destructive patterns and open the door to long-term consequences. Our goal is to think through the issues and take positive steps in our parenting to prepare our kids for what they will be facing.

Start Building the Relationship Early

Let us suggest that you *begin early to build a defense against unhealthy peer pressure*. And by early we mean *early!* If you intend to guard against this potentially dangerous influence, you'd better be at work long before your child enters his teen years.

One of the most important beginning steps a father can take is to *build a strong, wholesome relationship with your child from infancy.* If you are going to influence your child, you must make him an integral part of your life and you must become an important part of his. This includes a relationship that is marked by open and warm communication. The father who is consistently sarcastic, condemning or critical is chasing his children into the arms of their peers. If his verbal and non-verbal language is saying,

"Get away from me!"

"I don't have time for you or your problems!"

"I think you're stupid!"

"I don't like you!"

"I won't consider your views or feelings!"

he will alienate himself from his children and force them to search elsewhere for anything that will make them feel worthwhile and accepted.

Your problem might not be open rejection but neglect. In many cases, a well-intentioned dad's relationships with his kids weakens as they grow up, while their peer friendships deepen. In his book *The Effective Father,* author Gordon MacDonald writes:

> More than one family has coasted along with what the *parents* thought was a productive relational experience until a child reached middle adolescence. Suddenly — sometimes within weeks — breaks in communication occurred, new loyalties appeared, and a father and mother found themselves bewildered over the fact that their child seemed to be a new kind of human being.[1]

Due to Norm's own unhappy childhood, he determined to establish warm, compassionate, friendly relationships with his own children. He began at their birth and enjoyed their friendship through their childhood. On into their teen years, he continued to cultivate the friendships, spending time with each one, working on projects together, taking genuine interest in their thoughts, experiences and values. He is positive that those father-child experiences were foundational to his successful father-teen relationships.

Build Security and Self-confidence

Another action that neutralizes unhealthy peer influence is *building our children's sense of security and self-confidence,* strengthening their inner reserves. Our children's ultimate sense of security should be found in the Lord, but during their childhood years they will find that security in their relationship with you. The secure and self-confident child is less prone to manipulation by others.

The father-child relationship that nurtures security and confidence can also guide the child in forming strong convictions. If the child feels good about himself, his convictions will likely stand the test.

Challenge Negative Peer Pressure — Respectfully

We have another defense stategy available to us as parents. On the basis of a warm, positive relationship with our kids, we can *respectfully challenge unhealthy peer pressure.* We can let our kids know that many times it's in their best interest not to follow the crowd.

Norm's wife Winnie remembers how, when she was a teenager, she wanted a certain kind of saddle shoe that was popular at the time. When her parents would not buy her the "in" shoes because she had other shoes that were more than adequate, she grew angry and sulked. Her dad took her aside and challenged her to "dare to be different." He said, "Be who *God* called you to be. You don't have do what everyone else is doing. You're already a great person with or without those shoes." Because Winnie's relationship with and respect for her dad were strong, his counsel made a lifelong impression on her.

We should, however, be sensitive to our children when challenging the ways of their peers. Certain principles should guide our actions. First, let's underscore the basic tenet that we *respectfully* challenge unhealthy ideas or behaviors. Ridiculing or belittling your child's friends places him in an awkward situation: He may love you, but he has strong loyalties to his friends. If you attack the *person* of his friends, your child will try to defend them. He will probably do so by defending his friends' ideas or actions.

Second, when we challenge peer influence we should take the time and make the effort to *get clear, accurate information.* The dad who airs unfounded opinions, or who discredits ideas without clear evidence supporting his view, will lose his child's respect. If we are not certain about the facts, we should take the opportunity to seek them out with our children. We need never be afraid of the truth.

It is important that dads keep in tune with current issues that influence our children. When you read or hear something that you find relevant, you can share it with your child as a way to reinforce what you may be trying to teach.

John and his wife Pat were more than a little concerned when their son Rob mentioned that some of the guys on the baseball team had started using chewing tobacco.

"The boys were really putting pressure on the rest of the team to use the stuff," John relates. "When our son's closest friend Steve got hooked, my wife and I were worried about what the pressure would do to Rob.

"No amount of talking seemed to help. When we brought up the subject, Rob would get angry and not want to talk about it. It was obvious that Rob was both disappointed in his friend, and under the gun to conform to a habit some boys thought would make them look like big-leaguers.

"We were at a point where we weren't sure what we could do, when I happened across a magazine artile about a boy Rob's age who was dying of mouth cancer. The kid had gotten hooked on chewing tobacco and was paying a dear price for listening to his friends. There were even some graphic pictures showing the toll the disease had taken on this kid's face.

"I decided to lay the magazine on Rob's bed where he'd be sure to see it. A couple of evenings later Steve came over. I could hear them talking in Rob's bedroom.

"'Now do you see why I won't do that junk?' Rob asked.

"'Yeah . . .' Steve replied softly.

"The pressure on Rob eased up after that. He had been able to take a stand, backed up by more than just his mother's and my opinion."

John had helped his son stand up to negative peer pressure without a knock-down-drag-out fight, without demeaning Rob's friends. He simply took the time to be aware, and he cared enough to let his son know why he was concerned.

Check Your Motives

A final thought about neutralizing unhealthy peer pressure. *We need to be careful that we don't push our children into the arms of their peers.* It's likely to happen if we neglect our children. It's likely to happen if we engage in power struggles with them. It's likely to happen if we inadvertantly encourage our children to participate in questionable activities with their peers simply because we don't have the moral or spiritual courage to speak out against them.

Perhaps we don't want our children to be unpopular, so we decide to keep quiet. Or maybe *we* don't want to be unpopular with our children, their friends or the parents of their friends. Carefully evaluate the motives you have for talking (or not talking) with your kids about the influence of their peers.

Encouraging Positive Peer Relationships

One of the most effective options available to help us cope with unhealthy pressure is to steer our kids on a straight course by nurturing and supporting positive friendships.

Encourage Wise Selection of Friends

We'll highlight the obvious first: *We can encourage our children to form healthy relationships.* In their early years we can teach them to seek out friends who have good interpersonal habits, who speak wholesomely, who have godly convictions. Obviously younger children have not internalized their convictions, but they do reflect character traits that are good indicators of what their convictions will be.

The early chapters of Proverbs are Solomon's counsel to his son about establishing interpersonal relationships. This wise dad knew that he needed to point his son toward healthy relationships and give him knowledge about whom to seek out and whom to avoid. In like manner we can cultivate conversations with our children that help them identify healthy relationships.

A couple of years ago Dottie and I noticed that our son Sean was hanging around someone who had many bad habits–habits that would definitely lead to serious trouble down the road. The child's parents were not at all accessible to talk about it. As a result, I sat down with Sean and shared my concern. I decided to approach the subject by asking Sean what he thought about certain negative habits and actions. Immediately his response was, "That's not good."

Then I explained that what I had shared was true about a certain friend of Sean's, and that I was concerned about them spending a lot of time together. It worked. Soon they were not playing much together.

As I look back on that incident, I'm glad I didn't follow my first instinct to dictate that Sean stop playing with his friend. I also don't think I would have been effective had I lectured my son on his poor taste in friends. Rather, by explaining my concern and leaving the ball in Sean's court, he was able to make the wise choice.

Pray for Their Friendships

Second, *we can pray for our children* specifically in terms of their relationships. Many parents begin the day their child is born to pray consistently for the people who will influence that child's life. Who knows our children's needs and desires for positive friends better than the Lord? We encourage you to make a commitment to pray daily for your child and those who seek to influence him.

Form a Friendship Bond With Another Family

Third, *we can build family-to-family friendships.* Bob and Carole decided they needed to form a bond with another family for friendship, encouragement and fellowship. Prayerfully they thought through the families in their church, looking for those with loving, involved parents and well-adjusted kids of approximately the same ages as their own. Then they approached a couple and asked them to consider building an extended family relationship with them. They now spend an evening together twice a month sharing a meal, playing games and cultivating personal interaction. Their children have begun to develop bonds of friendship and they all have a lot of fun.

One family attended a church that didn't have any kids the same age as their son. With the blessing of their pastor, they began attending another church where healthy peer friendships could be established. These parents were wise to consider the importance of a positive peer group in their son's life and act upon it, rather than selfishly hang on to a church which could not meet the need of the whole family.

Be Realistic

A word of caution. Remember the earlier discussion about not being naive concerning what's happening in our children's lives? Too often Christian parents are naive about relationships among Christian youth. To assume that all the youth in your church are dedicated to Christ and living exemplary lives is unrealistic. There are needy people, individuals who have destructive habits and behaviors, in every church you visit. The girl your son dates may have an intense hunger to be affirmed, stroked and cherished. She may send signals to him that invite sexual activity. Or that fine young boy in the youth group may have difficulty controlling his sexual desires when he is alone with your daughter.

We are not suggesting that we be suspicious, negative parents. But we do need to be realistic, involved in our children's lives, knowing who they are hanging out with and how we can help them. So we would also strongly suggest that you commit to getting to know your children's friends on a personal level.

Peer pressure never goes away. But when we dads get lovingly involved in the lives of our kids, we can build an effective defense to help counteract the negative influences. By encouraging healthy friendships, through consistent prayer, and through enjoyable inter-family friendships, we can give our children solid foundations of acceptance, security and self-esteem from which they will make responsible choices.

● ● ●

FOR REFLECTION, DISCUSSION AND ACTION

1. How well do you know your child's friends? Think of one activity you can plan that would allow you to get to know your child's friends better in a non-threatening, fun atmosphere.

*2. Is your church meeting the social needs of your children? Do they have wholesome, encouraging peer groups to whom they can relate? Prayerfully consider whether your family will need to make a change.

3. How is today's peer pressure different from when you were a kid? How is it the same? What kind of pressures are your kids facing? (Why not ask them?)

*4. What one step can you and your wife take to reduce negative peer influence in your child's life? How will you avoid coming across as preachy or critical?

The Road to Self-Control
(Norm)

*E*d is a bright, talented twenty-four-year-old, who is a pastoral intern at a local church. While in seminary he hopes to grow in personal areas as well as in ministry skills.

The pastoral staff's initial impression of Ed was that he was intelligent and dedicated, and related well to people. After he had been with the church awhile, however, they noticed that he was consistently late for meetings.

When they talked about the problem, Ed confessed that he is helplessly defeated in self-discipline. His day begins at about 10 A.M. when he finally wakes up.

"Allyson wakes me before she leaves for work but I fall back asleep," he admitted. "Alarm clocks don't faze me. I just don't have the willpower to get out of bed."

"There's another issue," Ed continued. "I'm supposed to do visitation, but I procrastinate. I'm always scared someone will check up on me, but so far no one has asked about what I'm doing."

During Ed's internship with the church, the staff members concentrated on helping this young man establish self-discipline in his life. The task was difficult because his life-long habits and lack of willpower continued to work against him.

Ed's situation may be more extreme than some, but Josh and I constantly talk with men and women who are discouraged by their unfinished tasks, late deadlines and endless procrastination. Their lack of self-control affects other areas as well, and is manifested in a consistent pattern of unkept promises, sloppy homes or work areas, overeating, TV addiction, indulgence in sexual fantasy, or overspending ("How can I be out of money if I still have checks?").

Moving your children from parental control to self-control is another major task you face as a dad. *Self-control is one of the most valuable gifts you can give your child,* for your child's self-discipline or lack of same will determine his success in practically every area of his adolescent and adult life. Thus, we need to examine what is involved in the process of building self-control and discover how we can do so effectively and efficiently.

Begin at the Beginning

Teaching self-control is the act of *helping our children to make wise choices.* Think of it this way:

Step 1. You teach your child how to make wise choices.

Step 2. You guide him through the process as he makes wise choices.

Step 3. You reinforce these patterns of wise decision-making so that they become habits established in his thoughts and actions.

Step 1 concentrates on teaching, Step 2 on training, Step 3 on reinforcing.

Notice that we are talking about a long-term process that covers the first eighteen to twenty years of your child's life. We observe that most dads don't see the big picture or think in terms of a training process. Rather, they deal with difficult situations as isolated incidents instead of as parts of an overall plan for learning, building and growing.

To help you formulate an overall plan for encouraging self-control in your children, let's look at the three steps in more detail.

Step 1: Teaching

Deuteronomy 6:7 declares that parents are to *diligently* teach God's commandments to their children. The word picture in the original language is one of repeatedly sharpening an object. If our children are to make wise choices throughout life, we must begin by instilling principles of wisdom and decision-making in their early years and continue the process throughout their lives—sharpening, sharpening, sharpening. How do we do this effectively?

Determine What You Want Your Child to Know

What *information* does your child need to accumulate mentally early in life as a foundation for self-control and decision-making? What biblical truths will your child need by the time he is eighteen to give him a basis for choosing right from wrong—and the desire to choose right?

One truth that our children need to understand is that our lives are under the control of one of two forces. Jesus said, "No one can serve two masters. Either he will hate the one and love the other, or he will be devoted to the one and despise the other" (Matthew 6:24). The apostle Paul expanded on this fact when he wrote, "The sinful nature desires what is contrary to the

Spirit, and the Spirit what is contrary to the sinful nature. They are in conflict with each other, so that you do
not do what you want" (Romans 8:7).

To succeed as Christian men and women, all of
us must realize that true biblical self-control emerges
from God's direction of our lives through the empowering Holy Spirit. Galatians 5:22,23 lists self-control as one
of the "fruit of the Spirit," indicating that as we yield
our lives to God's direction, His Holy Spirit fills us with
the inner resources to honor God by living with discipline and diligence in all things.

Therefore, the non-optional starting point for
every dad is to be sure his own personal relationship with
God is solid, through an understanding of what it means
to be a Christian and what it means to be directed and
empowered by the Holy Spirit of God. We have provided
two appendices to help you in these areas: Appendix B,
"Would You Like to Know God Personally?" shows how
you can be certain Christ is in your life and that you are
living in His will. Appendix C, "Have You Made the
Wonderful Discovery of the Spirit-Filled Life?" shows
how some people get off track in their Christian lives,
and how to be directed and empowered by God through
His Holy Spirit on a daily basis. If you are personally
squared away on these two essential concepts, you will
have a supernatural inner source from which to live in
the power of our Lord Jesus Christ.

Josh and I also share the conviction that Christian dads should take the initiative to verbally guide
their children to a personal relationship with Christ.
Many of us seem to hope that our wives will take care of
these things or that if we just get our kids to Sunday
school the teachers will do the job for us. We may also
hope that if we read the Bible and pray as families our
children will become Christians by osmosis. Yet if we fail
to specifically show them how they can invite Jesus
Christ into their lives we neglect the most important

training point of all, the one with eternal significance.

Again, we suggest that you get to know the material in Appendix B, which has helped millions of individuals around the world receive Christ as Savior. Adapt it to the age of your child, then walk through the four principles with him and give him the opportunity to invite Jesus Christ into his life. If your child is not ready, don't push — he at least will know what to do when the time comes. (You may wish to read Bill Bright's excellent book *Witnessing Without Fear* for further help in sharing Christ with loved ones.)

There are undoubtedly other important truths and life-principles you and your wife want your children to learn. We suggest that you buy a notebook and take your wife out for coffee for a series of unhurried planning sessions. Here, you can share openly what dreams you have for the type of people you want your kids to become. You can determine together what your kids need to know in order to make wise choices and develop self-control. List the things that you want them to know about obedience, wisdom, problem-solving, honoring God, love and respect for members of the opposite sex, truthfulness and virtue.

This doesn't have to be an overwhelming task. Make it fun! Simply jot down the things that come to your minds. When you have a list, put one item at the top of each page, then brainstorm activities and ideas for how the two of you are going to work together to instill these truths and values in your children.

Make this type of interaction an ongoing process. (Not only will this help your parenting; you and your wife will draw closer together as you share dreams and agree on mutual goals and strategies.)

Observe Each of Your Children

Our children have to learn as *individuals*. Thus,

we need insight about each one. Ask yourself questions like these:

- What are the characteristics of this child's personality?
- What attitudes and behavior patterns have I observed that will influence his decision-making and self-control?
- What problems are unique to this child? (Insecure, prideful, people-pleaser, argumentative.)

As you observe your child, you will begin to discern the unique "bent" of his life and be able to nurture him in ways consistent with his personality. One child is more open and pliable; another is strong-willed, determined, resistant. You will want to work with each child's basic personality, not against it.

Jill is our middle child. She has lived under the shadow of an older sister and brother, both of whom are strong and assertive. During Jill's childhood years she was shy and hesitant.

I recall an evening during her high school years when Jill and I went for a walk after dinner. We discussed a close friend of the family who was going through emotional struggles, and as Jill shared her observations I was impressed with her wisdom and discernment.

In subsequent conversations I frequently noticed that she was very sensitive and insightful about people's behaviors and motivations. I began to tell Jill what I was observing—that she had a remarkable amount of wisdom for her age.

I believe those conversations affirmed positive qualities in Jill that she now values. They also were enjoyable occasions for Dad to express genuine respect for this shy family member.

Create a Teaching Environment

Busy fathers have to work smart at being effective dads. They look for natural opportunities to impart wisdom and insight.

Directed conversations at the evening meal can stimulate thinking and implant seeds of truth. This assumes, of course, that your family eats most evening and Sunday noon meals together. If you don't, why not? Well-adjusted young adults we've interviewed have told us that family mealtimes stand out as some of the most important "together" times in their childhood. If your family does not dine together regularly, we suggest you and your wife begin making it standard procedure again.

Meaningful conversations while driving to the store or working together on a project allow a natural exchange of ideas. Reading together can initiate conversations about important issues and allow you to explore principles of living as others apply them.

The environment of the home is a laboratory of daily living that allows you to observe your son or daughter and then impart the facts and ideas that you discern they need. And you needn't be a dad for long before you learn that home life also allows them to observe you, and how you exercise self-control in almost every type of situation.

Step 2: Training

One of the vital tasks your children face is to move from a position of absolute dependency as infants to that of self-control as adults. Our part in that process is to create the best learning environment that will enable them to work at building self-discipline for themselves. The training process includes imparting information; yet it goes beyond that to involve actually doing what is being taught. What guidelines, then, can we adopt to make practical training fruitful for our children?

Don't do for your children what they can more profitably do for themselves. It is easy for us to encourage dependency and leave our children crippled for life. The smart dad knows when his child is ready to assume new levels of responsibility for his own life, and he is eager to give him the opportunity to try out his wings.

Notice we've said to let your children do what they can *more profitably* do for themselves. We can do many things more efficiently or more accurately than our children, but it will not profit them. Many parents are too impatient or too perfectionistic to let their children have an opportunity to finish a task, so they step in and rescue their children, encouraging self-doubt and stunting the growth that comes from doing.

We need to create a secure environment in which our children can pursue a task, make mistakes and ask questions. Envision your home as your child's training site. You are the *guide* who comes alongside to encourage, support, correct and interact with him. The wise dad avoids a training approach that fosters guilt, anxiety or shame. He understands that self-control is more enhanced if it is built on positive reinforcement— strengthening the positive responses— rather than ridiculing mistakes or taking over to prevent mistakes.

Don't be afraid to hold your child accountable for what is realistic. When a quality father-child relationship exists, you can hold your child accountable for his actions and responsibilities without threatening his self-confidence. Your child knows he is secure and loved. He knows your concern for him is genuine. When you expect him to act responsibly he may chafe, but inwardly he will respect the fact that someone cares about his behavior and holds him to high standards.

When children have difficulty establishing self-control, parents need to be positive models of problem solving by offering realistic suggestions about what can be done. Ed, the defeated ministerial intern mentioned earlier, didn't have much help from his parents in developing self-control. He told the church staff team that his parents had required nothing of him. They always made his decisions for him, regularly got him up in the morning and never assigned him chores around the house. Making life so easy for their son was actually a terrible disservice to him.

Model Self-Control

An effective training process allows the trainee to observe the trainer doing what he (the trainee) will eventually be doing. The trainer carefully describes what he does and why he does it that way. The trainee thus moves from books, ideas and theories to practical application in real life.

Remember, we can't expect our children to function on the same level of accomplishment we do. They need time to gain proficiency; the best thing we can do is be patient and allow their proficiency to emerge. We can help our children set attainable goals, lovingly hold them to those goals and affirm them when they have reached their goals.

As parents, modeling accountability to each other and to our children indicates the importance of a life of self-control. For example, if you have an argument with your children's mother in front of them, you not only need to ask your wife for forgiveness, but, because your children were observers, you need to ask them for forgiveness. This lets your kids know how highly you value doing the right thing.

Being accountable to our kids is fertile training ground for them to be far more willing to be accountable to us, others and especially their heavenly Father.

Step 3: Reinforcing

As our children take each step toward personal self-discipline we must consistently reinforce their actions with praise and encouragement. *More is gained by reinforcing positive steps of personal control than by criticizing failure.* In other words, (to adapt a good management strategy) *catch your children doing something right.* Strengthen the lesson with affirmation and appropriate praise. This will not only reinforce what they achieve but will *increase their motivation* to undertake areas where self-control is still weak. Your child needs consistent encouragement. Commit yourself to being a positive dad.

Adjust Your Plan

One of the best ways to motivate your child to self-control is to grant him new privileges appropriate to his emerging growth. This is exactly what our heavenly Father does. We read in Hebrews 12 that "God disciplines us for our good, that we may share in His holiness" (verse 10). Sharing in His holiness is our Father's way of saying, "You're growing up. You're maturing. I want to enrich your life more."

Some parents are rigidly consistent—they treat a child fundamentally the same when he is sixteen as when he was six. Their approach is to control the child until he leaves the home. Often this child feels so smothered, hemmed in and stifled that he reacts by unwise and unhealthy overindulgence. Not only has he never learned the life of self-control, but he also has come to emotionally despise *any* control.

By contrast, the wise father adapts the training process to his child and quickly opens new doors of opportunity as he sees growth. He discerns when the child is ready for a new challenge, responsibility or privilege and extends it in a way that it becomes both an incentive and a positive affirmation of trust.

Self-Control and Sexual Expression

When functioning properly, self-control and sexual expression operate as two dynamics, enriching each other. When one is warped or diseased, the other will be affected. When we nurture self-restraint in our children, they feel better about themselves. They know they have a handle on their lives and are not being victimized by personal cravings that run wild. This in turn stimulates self-respect and a sense of personal dignity that allows them to relate positively with others. Consequently our children's sexuality is not chained to uncontrolled desires that could twist and distort their sexual expression through destructive behaviors. Our children live with us in a misguided and undisciplined society. Dangerous traps that endeavor to exploit their lives exist in every direction. Our children can easily be exploited, seduced and corrupted by a world view that equates sexuality with sexual promiscuity. The child of God who is able to exercise self-control, empowered by God's Holy Spirit, will live an enriched, joyful, fruitful life.

● ● ●

FOR REFLECTION, DISCUSSION AND ACTION

1. On a scale of 1 to 10, rate yourself in the area of self-control. Consider how you respond in a crisis, in an argument, in a tempting situation, and in matters of eating and other personal habits. If you gave yourself a 7 or better, to what factors do you attribute your success in this area? If you rated yourself 6 or below, why do you think self-control is a problem for you? What have you learned from this exercise that will help you instill this character quality in each of your children?

*2. With your wife (or with a close friend if you're a single dad), spend an hour or two listing the key truths and values you want your children to learn. Then decide on at least one strategy or activity you can begin to implement to help teach each truth or value.

*3. Carefully, prayerfully, study Appendices B and C at the end of this book. Take any steps you feel the Lord is directing you to take.

Dad,
You Can Do It!
(Josh and Norm)

Charlie Shedd coined the term in his 1975 book, *Smart Dads I Know*. A smart dad was one who overcame the common and uncommon obstacles that might have prevented him from being a good, caring dad to his kids.

The challenges we men face demand that we be smart dads. Fathering has been a complex task in every generation, but in the 20th century the job of fatherhood taxes our resources and stretches our imagination to the limit.

The good news is that the man who says "I'm dedicated to being an effective Christian father" has undertaken a quest that will result in as much growth in him as it will in his child. That is one of the genuinely exciting aspects of fathering!

The Right Attitude

God's Word teaches us that "as a man thinks in his heart, so is he." Your mental attitude sets you up to either move forward optimistically or to hesitate, seeing every problem as an enemy trying to torpedo your ship. A positive mental attitude is crucial for handling the unique circumstances and personal limitations that may come your way in fathering.

If you haven't done so yet, decide now that you are going to face fathering with true biblical optimism. The apostle Paul said, "I can do *everything* through him who gives me strength" (Philippians 4:13). That includes being an effective, godly dad in demanding situations.

The Bible says that our loving Father oversees every aspect of our lives. He knows our circumstances and He wants to use these very situations to strengthen us and stimulate us to the full stature of men of God. So whatever your roadblocks, limitations or situations, consider them opportunities for growth. It is our conviction that fathering is one of the key ways the Lord will bring us to maturity. That's reason enough to be optimistic.

Often our mental attitude is not as positive as it could be because we think of parenting in terms of *my* responsibility, *my* skills, *my* knowledge. We lose sight of the Lord's commitment to participate in every facet of our lives. But when we think in terms of seeking *His* wisdom, *His* strength, *His* love, *His* patience, *His* compassion, our perspective changes. We can be genuinely excited about what *He* is going to do. Our part is to walk with Him through the fathering experience, anticipating His active, faithful participation.

Let's summarize these thoughts in three statements:

1. My mental attitude determines my success as a dad.

2. Fathering is an opportunity for significant growth in my life.

3. The challenges of fathering lead me to discover the vastness and reality of God's resources for my own life.

It's *smart* to have a positive attitude!

Face Up to Your Special Challenges

At times fathering is very hard work. It may even be painful. But we believe that the difficulty and pain of fatherhood is not something to fear. In all our weakness, in our special calling as dads, we can discover the Lord's enabling and ultimately grow through our experiences. The hard work and pain eventually pays off!

Many dads face situations that are so intense and demanding that they merit discussion here. You may find yourself in a difficult situation because of choices you made; or you may be overwhelmed by circumstances beyond your control. Either way, to be an effective father you'll want to face the problem honestly and make any changes that are necessary.

The Overworked Dad

When Norm was in college one of his friends, a native of India, said to him, "When I lived in India I thought that Americans were rich, lazy people who sat around doing nothing. But when I arrived in the States, I discovered that I was greatly mistaken. You work hard — sometimes too hard!"

In our grandfather's generation men labored physically. Today a man's labor is more likely to be mentally and emotionally demanding. He faces time deadlines, the pressures of filling weekly or monthly quotas, and the mental stresses associated with an electronic world and a fast-paced life. If you're like many dads, you probably find yourself coming home at the end of a workday mentally and emotionally exhausted, still thinking about what went on today and what's going to happen tomorrow. And many of us work well beyond the forty-hour week. In many cases, we leave ourselves limited reserves for parenting.

In addition to our jobs, most of us have other interests that compete with our families for our time.

Sports, hobbies, home maintenance, church activities, community involvement, and a host of other activities vie for our attention.

If you're an overcommitted dad, your challenge is twofold. First, you need to *reevaluate your personality and priorities.* Perhaps you feel more significant, or even more secure, if you are busy. Are you overcommitted *because you want it that way?* Or have you failed to set priorities to determine, from a Christian perspective, what is most significant in your life? You may be uncomfortable grappling with these questions. They may even be threatening. But it's important to realize that ignoring these questions may cause irreparable damage in your relationship with your children.

A man's priorities are put to the test when he is offered a lucrative job advancement which conflicts with the needs of family members. Ray is such a man. At a men's retreat he related the following incident:

"The company vice president called me into his office and told me that I was to be promoted to a new position. It would mean that our family would relocate in another city, and I would have additional responsibilities. Initially I was thrilled because I never could resist a new challenge.

"As with every important decision I've been faced with, I began to seek God's direction. When I committed this opportunity to Him, He helped me see that it would not be healthy for our family. My relationship with my two sons is so fulfilling that I knew I couldn't give it second place to a job.

"It was hard to decline the promotion, knowing I might not get another chance like this again. But in my heart I knew I'd made the right choice."

Ray's a smart dad!

The second challenge for the busy dad is to *work*

smart. For example, Neil is a salesman who travels within his state. He frequently has to be away from home Monday through Friday. When Neil has a week like that, he makes sure that Saturday is family day. His children look forward to that day knowing they'll have the full attention of their dad.

The smart dad who is busy looks for ways to make the maximum use of briefer time periods. A twenty-minute walk with your daughter can accomplish much if you give her your full attention during that time. Twenty minutes of one-on-one basketball in the driveway with your son before dinner can be as good for the relationship as for your heart and waistline. A regular family dinner time—with the TV and telephone *off*—can be a haven of warm, cheerful conversation for every family member.

Busy dads can still be good dads—but we have to be smart!

The Divorced Dad

Perhaps your fathering has been affected by a divorce. Divorce weakens—and sometimes severs—the relationship between father and child. In the majority of cases the children continue to live with their mother. If she is bitter or hostile toward their father, the father's relationship with the children can be strained even further. Many dads find it difficult to maintain a meaningful relationship with their children through infrequent contacts.

A crucial warning for divorced dads and moms: Never put your children in the middle of your problems. If one parent expresses resentment toward the other parent, the child is likely to reflect the same resentment.

Family, marriage and child counselor Dick Day told us how a divorced mother came for counseling about her thirteen-year-old daughter. The dad had left the family when the mom was pregnant with this girl, and now the teen was extremely bitter toward her father.

Dick asked the mother how much time the daughter had spent with her dad in the past thirteen years. She estimated about two months. Dick immediately confronted the mother: "The feelings your daughter has toward her father could not have come from those two months of exposure to him. I suspect that those feelings toward her dad have come from you, not her experience."

The woman went home to think about it, then returned the following week. "You're right," she told Dick. "I've been force-feeding my own resentment to my daughter, and it's been harmful to her. I've got to be more positive about her father."

We know divorced dads who have accepted the challenge, weathered the trying times and continued to have significant positive influence on their children. These dads think and act smart.

Smart divorced dads plan thoughtfully and creatively. Rex is such a man. He has two daughters; one was eleven and the other thirteen when the divorce occurred. Even though Rex had to work through his own emotional pain, he consistently affirmed his love and commitment to the girls—nothing spectacular, just genuine fatherly love and care. When they were with him on Saturdays he spent time with them, working together and doing things they liked. In time his ex-wife realized that she couldn't care for their children, and they went to live with Rex, who by this time had remarried. Today both girls have more stable lives because of a dad who wouldn't quit when the going got tough.

Divorced dads can better nourish their children if they themselves are living healthy, fulfilled lives. When emptiness, boredom or resentment are in control, they seep out, infecting those around us. The man who has personal challenges, who maintains close personal friendships through support groups and who focuses his energy on caring for others will be a more positive model for his children to follow.

The Stepdad

A new term in our 20th century vocabulary is the *blended family*. It refers to those families who have children in the home from a previous marriage. Let's think for a few minutes about the problems of step-parenting.

Your stepchild may resent your infringing on what he feels is his personal territory—his mother. He perceives you as someone vying for his mother's attention and affection. He also will likely resent your efforts to give leadership in his life. He may wonder how much authority you legitimately have over him because you're not really his dad. And, even if he likes you, he is caught in a loyalty crisis—to accept you or to be friendly to you may seem to him like a betrayal of his own father.

Establishing a good, fruitful relationship as a stepdad is not an overnight process. We've noticed that the stepdad who is willing to "go the second mile" may have the joy of ministering to the child in a powerful way. We have also observed stepparent-child relationships that have been strong, warm and lasting. We'd like to share some general guidelines to help you as a stepdad.

Remember that blending takes time. Children need time to sort out their feelings and become open to a relationship with you. If you move too quickly into the relationship, or endeavor to establish strong authority over the child, he will likely back away. Give the child time to get to know you, to establish a trust relationship, to work through his turbulent feelings.

We have observed that in many blended-family situations the following sequence unfolds:

1. Initial acceptance by the child: "I like him. Marry him." The woman's kids may feel that whatever makes Mom happy is fine.

2. The end of the honeymoon for the child: "I don't like you! You're not my dad! I won't do what you ask me to do!" It is important that you not be discouraged or overwhelmed at this stage. Remember that the child may have many unclear emotions stirring within him. You may be the object of his anger toward his natural father. Or he may be testing you to see if you *really* care about him. Your continued compassion, patience and openness are likely to win out in the end.

3. Acceptance by the child on a tested, confident basis: The child knows you really care about him as a person, no matter what he does or whose child he is.

The Deficient Dad

All of us belong to this group, though we don't feel comfortable talking about it. But here, too, we discover smart dads who know how to accept the challenge of their imperfections, inadequacies and limitations.

Some men have *personality limitations* that reduce their fathering effectiveness. As long as Al can remember, he has had a deep-rooted anger that leaks out in both verbal and non-verbal communication. Karl feels defeated because he can never say no to anyone and puts his family second to everyone else's wants. He suffers from a lot of guilt. Paul grew up being the community wimp and has always felt ashamed that he isn't more courageous.

Other men have *skill limitations*. They honestly don't know how to be competent fathers. Mark is an outstanding CPA and highly respected by his peers, but talk to him about his children and his face drops. "I think I'm blowing it and I don't know what to do," he sighs.

One common lament we've heard during the many parenting seminars we've conducted over the years is, "I wish I'd learned these things when our children were younger. I've done so many dumb things."

One reason many men lack fathering skills is because they didn't have a positive model to follow. Many men grew up in fatherless homes. Others grew up in homes where dad was largely an absent family member because of work, outside interests or neglect. And our impersonal society greatly reduces the opportunity for children to find adult role models outside the home. Many fathers were never shown what good fathering was all about. Our prayer is that this book will help to fill that void.

Limitations Are Growth Opportunities

Let's face it honestly: We all have personal limitations. The Christian life is a life of growth. It is God's call to each of us to find new liberation from enslaving sins and habit patterns that have robbed us of joy and fruitfulness. If we are honest with ourselves, we must admit that our weaknesses and failures in fathering are calling us to deal with personal growth issues. We can deny them, or see them as invitations to grow into the godly men, husbands and fathers God has called us to be.

We believe that life is a special gift from our loving Father. God's redemption, offered through Jesus Christ, is His clear signal that He wants to accomplish a powerful transformation within us. His resources are readily available. All He wants is our response to Him as He calls us to His side where He can love, instruct, enrich, free and bless us. Parenting is one practical setting in which He can work this out.

You have your special set of circumstances, your unique strengths and weaknesses. Let fathering be that life situation in which you commit yourself to becoming the man of God the Lord has called you to be. Not only will your own life become more satisfying, but you will also pass on to your sons and daughters a genuine hunger and thirst for righteousness. And this would indeed be the greatest gift you could ever leave them.

● ● ●

FOR REFLECTION, DISCUSSION AND ACTION

1. Assess your general attitude toward the challenges of fathering your kids. Is it positive, negative or somewhere in between? Explain the reason for your answer.

2. How would your wife assess your attitude toward the challenges of fathering? Your kids? Explain your answer.

3. Write out and memorize a completion for this statement: "Being a loving, involved dad to my kids is a positive experience for me because . . . "

*4. What two concepts stood out most to you from this chapter? Explain why they caught your attention, and what action you intend to take to integrate them into your life.

*5. Find a quiet place and invest ten to twenty minutes writing out a completion to this statement: "As a result of reading, thinking about and discussing this book, I intend to . . . " Be as specific and thorough as possible. Then share what you've written with your group. When all have shared, join together in prayer that God would help you implement the action points you've written. If you are not in a group, share what you've written with your wife or with a trusted friend.

Appendix A

Fun Things Dads Can Do With Their Kids

Have a "Date With Dad" once every three months with each of your children.

Hold a Sunday-afternoon Family Board Games marathon.

Take a walk through the neighborhood at Christmas to see the lights.

Do a basic home or car repair job together.

Cook up a special meal for Mom. Have the kids make menus, and everyone serves as a waiter or waitress. (And clean up afterward!)

Go to breakfast together. Let your child order for you.

Build a model together . . . but let your child do most of the actual work.

Take a nature hike.

Go camping overnight or for the full weekend.

Bake a major batch of chocolate chip cookies to distribute to your child's friends.

Get two inexpensive cameras and lots of film. Do photo shoots together on walks, at the zoo, around the house, etc. Select photos and work together on a scrapbook.

Select key Scripture verses and memorize them together, discussing what each verse means to you. Reward each other with frozen yogurt each time you both can quote ten new verses word-perfect.

Have a croquet or badminton tournament in your backyard.

Go to your child's athletic or special activities—encourage and praise (but don't be a pushy "Little League Parent"!)

Say, "I want to be praying for you this week. What's on your mind—what would you like me to pray about?"

Design and plant a flower garden together.

Make a basket of fresh fruit, breads, gourmet crackers and canned goods and leave it on the porch of a needy family.

Ask, "What's the best thing that happened to you today?"

Ask your children to pray for you.

Put together a surprise "This Is Your Life" program for Mom or for the grandparents.

Tell your kids why you love their mother. Have them tell you why they love her. Then get a piece of poster board and join the kids in writing all these reasons on a giant greeting card with crayon. Have the kids decorate and deliver the card to Mom.

Join with one or two other families for a family skit and talent night, with everyone participating. Rent a video camera to record the event for posterity.

At dinner, have everyone share about "My Most Embarrassing Moment."

With 3 x 5 cards, staple together a handmade coupon book for each child. Each coupon entitles them to a one-on-one date with Dad for ice cream, a ball game, bowling or roller skating, a game of their choice, pizza, etc. Suggested rule: Limit one coupon per month per child.

Read through a book of the Bible together, discussing it as you go.

Go to a local or country museum.

Pick out a cologne for Mom that you all like.

Find an apple or cherry orchard and arrange a day of picking with your kids.

Check your city for free outdoor concerts or plays in the park. Fix a picnic and make an evening of it.

Take a trip to the library. Get each child a library card and help them discover the world of good books.

Buy or rent an aerobics video and work out together.

Go to plays and concerts staged by local colleges and universities.

Go for a series of family bike rides.

Go fly a kite.

Walk to construction sites and watch the progress on a building, house or road.

If your children have surviving grandparents, have a "Grandparents Appreciation Day" with homemade cards, crafts and goodies made by you and the kids. Then do the same for Mom, then for a neighbor or friend, then for your pastor or youth pastor.

Put together a jigsaw puzzle.

After family dinner, back the chairs away from the table and play "Concentration," that favorite old parlor game where players number off, then slap knees twice, clap hands twice, and call out their number and someone else's number as they snap their fingers. Then everyone pitches in to clean up the kitchen; the winner gets to choose his task.

Get on the floor and watch your young child's favorite TV program with him.

Pick flowers from the garden and assemble a bouquet for Mom or another special person.

By yourself, pick flowers and assemble a bouquet for your daughter.

Build a bookshelf or soap box racer with your son.

Have a candlelight night. Turn out all the lights, light candles and build a fire, pop popcorn, and sit around telling favorite stories.

Pray together for special people in your lives.

Call ahead, then take a tour of the local fire station.

Blow bubbles in the backyard.

At Christmas, Easter, Independence Day, etc., put on plays with your children to dramatize the meaning of the holiday.

For each child's twelfth birthday, give him a jar with fifty-two "Special Treat" slips. Your child can draw one per week. Include simple treats as well as more elaborate. For example: "Stay up an hour later one night this week." "Invite a friend to spend the night." "Go to Baskin-Robbins with Dad for ice cream."

Serve together in some community or church project. Serve food at a homeless shelter or volunteer to help in the church nursery.

Take community school classes together: photography, woodworking, basic auto mechanics or home repair, etc.

Write letters to shut-ins from your church, or visit local nursing homes with a puppy for the patients to cuddle.

Begin reading C.S. Lewis's *The Chronicles of Narnia* together.

Surprise your child by picking him up at school and take him to a movie, for a picnic or pizza, etc.

Arrange to have lunch with your young child at school.

Plan a "Hidden Supper." Hide quick-fix items throughout the house, and give a clue to where the first item is located. Second clue is found with the first item, and so on. Fix the food items together.

Have an "Honor Night" for each family member. Prepare that person's special food, have a special place of honor at the table, design an honor plaque, and have each family member share "What I appreciate about . . . "

Once a month, plan a formal dinner. Everyone dresses up, and the table is spread with the fancy china. Use this fun occasion to teach etiquette.

Would You Like to Know God Personally?

The following four principles will help you discover how to know God personally and experience the abundant life He promised.

1 GOD **LOVES** YOU AND CREATED YOU TO KNOW HIM PERSONALLY.

(References contained in these pages should be read in context from the Bible whenever possible.)

God's Love

"For God so loved the world, that He gave His only begotten Son, that whoever believes in Him should not perish, but have eternal life" (John 3:16).

God's Plan

"Now this is eternal life: that they may know you, the only true God, and Jesus Christ, whom you have sent" (John 17:3, NIV).

What prevents us from knowing God personally?

2 MAN IS **SINFUL** AND **SEPARATED** FROM GOD, SO WE CANNOT KNOW HIM PERSONALLY OR EXPERIENCE HIS LOVE.

Man Is Sinful

"For all have sinned and fall short of the glory of God" (Romans 3:23).

Man was created to have fellowship with God; but, because of his stubborn self-will, he chose to go his own independent way, and fellowship with God was broken. This self-will, characterized by an attitude of active rebellion or passive indifference, is evidence of what the Bible calls sin.

Man Is Separated

"For the wages of sin is death" (spiritual separation from God) (Romans 6:23).

HOLY GOD

↑↑↑↑

SINFUL MAN

This diagram illustrates that God is holy and man is sinful. A great gulf separates the two. The arrows illustrate that man is continually trying to reach God and establish a personal relationship with Him through his own efforts, such as a good life, philosophy or religion.

The third principle explains the only way to bridge this gulf . . .

3 JESUS CHRIST IS GOD'S **ONLY** PROVISION FOR MAN'S SIN. THROUGH HIM ALONE WE CAN KNOW GOD PERSONALLY AND EXPERIENCE HIS LOVE.

He Died in Our Place

"But God demonstrates His own love toward us, in that while we were yet sinners, Christ died for us" (Romans 5:8).

He Rose From the Dead

"Christ died for our sins . . . He was buried . . . He was raised on the third day, according to the Scriptures . . . He appeared to Peter, then to the twelve. After that He appeared to more than five hundred" (1 Corinthians 15:3-6).

He Is the Only Way to God

"Jesus said to him, 'I am the way, and the truth, and the life; no one comes to the Father, but through Me' " (John 14:6).

This diagram illustrates that God has bridged the gulf which separates us from Him by sending His Son, Jesus Christ, to die on the cross in our place to pay the penalty for our sins.

GOD
JESUS
MAN

It is not enough just to know these truths...

4 WE MUST INDIVIDUALLY **RECEIVE** JESUS CHRIST AS SAVIOR AND LORD; THEN WE CAN KNOW GOD PERSONALLY AND EXPERIENCE HIS LOVE.

We Must Receive Christ

"But as many as received Him, to them He gave the right to become children of God, even to those who believe in His name" (John 1:12).

We Receive Christ Through Faith

"For by grace you have been saved through faith; and that not of yourselves, it is the gift of God; not as a result of works, that no one should boast" (Ephesians 2:8,9).

When We Receive Christ, We Experience a New Birth. (Read John 3:1-8.)

We Receive Christ by Personal Invitation

(Christ is speaking): "Behold, I stand at the door and knock; if anyone hears My voice and opens the door, I will come in to him" (Revelation 3:20).

Receiving Christ involves turning to God from self (repentance) and trusting Christ to come into our lives to forgive our sins and to make us the kind of people He wants us to be. Just to agree intellectually that Jesus Christ is the Son of God and that He died on the cross for our sins is not enough. Nor is it enough to have an emotional experience. We receive Jesus Christ by faith, as an act of the will.

These two circles represent two kinds of lives:

SELF-DIRECTED LIFE
S – Self is on the throne
† – Christ is outside the life
● – Interests are directed by self, often resulting in discord and frustration

CHRIST-DIRECTED LIFE
† – Christ is in the life and on the throne
S – Self is yielding to Christ
● – Interests are directed by Christ, resulting in harmony with God's plan

Which circle best represents your life? Which circle would you like to have represent your life?

The following explains how you can invite Jesus Christ into your life:

YOU CAN RECEIVE CHRIST RIGHT NOW BY FAITH THROUGH PRAYER

(Prayer is talking with God)

God knows your heart and is not so concerned with your words as He is with the attitude of your heart. The following is a suggested prayer:

> "Lord Jesus, I want to know You personally. Thank You for dying on the cross for my sins. I open the door of my life and receive You as my Savior and Lord. Thank You for forgiving my sins and giving me eternal life. Take control of the throne of my life. Make me the kind of person You want me to be."

Does this prayer express the desire of your heart?

If it does, pray this prayer right now, and Christ will come into your life, as He promised.

How to Know That Christ Is in Your Life

Did you receive Christ into your life? According to His promise in Revelation 3:20, where is Christ right now in relation to you? Christ said that He would come into your life and be your friend so you can know Him personally. Would He mislead you? On what authority do you know that God has answered your prayer? (The trustworthiness of God Himself and His Word.)

The Bible Promises Eternal Life to All Who Receive Christ

"And the witness is this, that God has given us eternal life, and this life is in His Son. He who has the Son has the life; he who does not have the Son of God does not have the life. These things I have written to you who believe in the name of the Son of God, in order that you may know that you have eternal life" (1 John 5:11-13).

Thank God often that Christ is in your life and that He will never leave you (Hebrews 13:5). You can know on the basis of His promise that Christ lives in you and that you have eternal life, from the very moment you invite Him in. He will not deceive you.

An important reminder . . .

DO NOT DEPEND ON FEELINGS

The promise of God's Word, the Bible — not our feelings — is our authority. The Christian lives by faith (trust) in the trustworthiness of God Himself and His Word. This train diagram illustrates the relationship between fact (God and His Word), faith (our trust in God and His Word), and feeling (the result of our faith and obedience) (John 14:21).

The train will run with or without the caboose. However, it would be useless to attempt to pull the train by the caboose. In the same way, we, as Christians, do not depend on feelings or emotions, but we place our faith (trust) in the trustworthiness of God and the promises of His Word.

Fellowship in a Good Church

God's Word admonishes us not to forsake "the assembling of ourselves together" (Hebrews 10:25). Several logs burn brightly together, but put one aside on the cold hearth and the fire goes out. So it is with your relationship with other Christians. If you do not belong to a church, do not wait to be invited. Take the initiative; call the pastor of a nearby church where Christ is honored and His Word is preached. Start this week, and make plans to attend regularly.

Suggestions for Christian Growth

Spiritual growth results from trusting Jesus Christ. "The righteous man shall live by faith" (Galatians 3:11). A life of faith will enable you to trust God increasingly with every detail of your life.

* * * * *

Steven Pogue has written an excellent book designed to help you make the most of your new life in Christ. The title is **The First Year of Your Christian Life**, and it is available in Christian bookstores everywhere, or you can call 1-800-950-4HLP to order directly from the publisher.

Have You Made the Wonderful Discovery of the Spirit-Filled Life?

EVERY DAY CAN BE AN EXCITING ADVENTURE FOR THE CHRISTIAN who knows the reality of being filled with the Holy Spirit and who lives constantly, moment by moment, under His gracious direction.

The Bible tells us that there are three kinds of people:

1. NATURAL MAN

(One who has not received Christ)

"But a natural man does not accept the things of the Spirit of God; for they are foolishness to him, and he cannot understand them, because they are spiritually appraised" (1 Corinthians 2:14).

SELF-DIRECTED LIFE

S - Ego or finite self is on the throne
† - Christ is outside the life
● - Interests are directed by self, often resulting in discord and frustration

2. SPIRITUAL MAN

(One who is directed and empowered by the Holy Spirit)

"But he who is spiritual appraises all things . . ." (1 Corinthians 2:15).

CHRIST-DIRECTED LIFE

† - Christ is in the life and on the throne
S - Self is yielding to Christ
● - Interests are directed by Christ, resulting in harmony with God's plan

3. CARNAL MAN

(One who has received Christ, but who lives in defeat because he trusts in his own efforts to live the Christian life)

"And I, brethren, could not speak to you as to spiritual men, but as to carnal men, as to babes in Christ. I gave you milk to drink, not solid food; for you were not yet able to receive it. Indeed, even now you are not yet able, for you are still carnal. For since there is jealousy and strife among you, are you not fleshly, and are you not walking like mere men?" (1 Corinthians 3:1-3)

SELF-DIRECTED LIFE

S - Self is on the throne
† - Christ dethroned and not allowed to direct the life
● - Interests are directed by self, often resulting in discord and frustration

1 GOD HAS PROVIDED FOR US AN ABUNDANT AND FRUITFUL CHRISTIAN LIFE.

Jesus said, "I came that they might have life, and might have it abundantly" (John 10:10).

"I am the vine, you are the branches; he who abides in Me, and I in him, he bears much fruit; for apart from Me you can do nothing" (John 15:5).

"But the fruit of the Spirit is love, joy, peace, patience, kindness, goodness, faithfulness, gentleness, self-control; against such things there is no law" (Galatians 5:22,23).

"But you shall receive power when the Holy Spirit has come upon you; and you shall be My witnesses both in Jerusalem, and in all Judea and Samaria, and even to the remotest part of the earth" (Acts 1:8).

THE SPIRITUAL MAN — Some personal traits which result from trusting God:

Christ-centered
Empowered by the Holy Spirit
Introduces others to Christ
Effective prayer life
Understands God's Word
Trusts God
Obeys God
Love
Joy
Peace
Patience
Kindness
Faithfulness
Goodness

The degree to which these traits are manifested in the life depends upon the extent to which the Christian trusts the Lord with every detail of his life, and upon his maturity in Christ. One who is only beginning to understand the ministry of the Holy Spirit should not be discouraged if he is not as fruitful as more mature Christians who have known and experienced this truth for a longer period.

Why is it that most Christians are not experiencing the abundant life?

2 CARNAL CHRISTIANS CANNOT EXPERIENCE THE ABUNDANT AND FRUITFUL CHRISTIAN LIFE.

The carnal man trusts in his own efforts to live the Christian life:

A. He is either uninformed about, or has forgotten, God's love, forgiveness and power (Romans 5:8-10; Hebrews 10:1-25; 1 John 1; 2:1-3; 2 Peter 1:9; Acts 1:8).

B. He has an up-and-down spiritual experience.

C. He cannot understand himself — he wants to do what is right, but cannot.

D. He fails to draw upon the power of the Holy Spirit to live the Christian life (1 Corinthians 3:1-3; Romans 7:15-24; 8:7; Galatians 5:16-18).

THE CARNAL MAN — Some or all of the following traits may characterize the Christian who does not fully trust God:

Ignorance of his spiritual heritage
Unbelief
Disobedience
Loss of love for God and for others
Poor prayer life
No desire for Bible study
Legalistic attitude
Impure thoughts
Jealousy
Guilt
Worry
Discouragement
Critical spirit
Frustration
Aimlessness

(The individual who professes to be a Christian but who continues to practice sin should realize that he may not be a Christian at all, according to 1 John 2:3; 3:6,9; Ephesians 5:5.)

The third truth gives us the only solution to this problem . . .

3 JESUS PROMISED THE ABUNDANT AND FRUITFUL LIFE AS THE RESULT OF BEING FILLED (DIRECTED AND EMPOWERED) BY THE HOLY SPIRIT.

The Spirit-filled life is the Christ-directed life by which Christ lives His life in and through us in the power of the Holy Spirit (John 15).

A. One becomes a Christian through the ministry of the Holy Spirit, according to John 3:1-8. From the moment of spiritual birth, the Christian is indwelt by the Holy Spirit at all times (John 1:12; Colossians 2:9,10; John 14:16,17).

Though all Christians are indwelt by the Holy Spirit, not all Christians are filled (directed and empowered) by the Holy Spirit on an ongoing basis.

B. The Holy Spirit is the source of the overflowing life (John 7:37-39).

C. The Holy Spirit came to glorify Christ (John 16:1-15). When one is filled with the Holy Spirit, he is a true disciple of Christ.

D. In His last command before His ascension, Christ promised the power of the Holy Spirit to enable us to be witnesses for Him (Acts 1:1-9).

How, then, can one be filled with the Holy Spirit?

4 WE ARE FILLED (DIRECTED AND EMPOWERED) BY THE HOLY SPIRIT BY FAITH; THEN WE CAN EXPERIENCE THE ABUNDANT AND FRUITFUL LIFE WHICH CHRIST PROMISED TO EACH CHRISTIAN.

You can appropriate the filling of the Holy Spirit **right now** if you:

A. Sincerely desire to be directed and empowered by the Holy Spirit (Matthew 5:6; John 7:37-39).

B. Confess your sins. By **faith** thank God that He **has** forgiven all of your sins—past, present and future—because Christ died for you (Colossians 2:13-15; 1 John 1; 2:1-3; Hebrews 10:1-17).

C. Present every area of your life to God (Romans 12:1,2).

D. By **faith** claim the fullness of the Holy Spirit, according to:

1. HIS COMMAND—Be filled with the Spirit. "And do not get drunk with wine, for that is dissipation, but be filled with the Spirit" (Ephesians 5:18).

2. HIS PROMISE—He will always answer when we pray according to His will. "And this is the confidence which we have before Him, that, if we ask any-thing according to His will, He hears us. And if we know that He hears us in whatever we ask, we know that we have the requests which we have asked from Him" (1 John 5:14,15).

Faith can be expressed through prayer...

How to Pray in Faith to be Filled With the Holy Spirit

We are filled with the Holy Spirit by **faith** alone. However, true prayer is one way of expressing your faith. The following is a suggested prayer:

> "Dear Father, I need You. I acknowledge that I have been directing my own life and that, as a result, I have sinned against You. I thank You that You have forgiven my sins through Christ's death on the cross for me. I now invite Christ to again take His place on the throne of my life. Fill me with the Holy Spirit as You **commanded** me to be filled, and as You **promised** in Your Word that You would do if I asked in faith. I pray this in the name of Jesus. As an expression of my faith, I now thank You for directing my life and for filling me with the Holy Spirit."

Does this prayer express the desire of your heart? If so, bow in prayer and trust God to fill you with the Holy Spirit **right now.**

How to Know That You Are Filled (Directed and Empowered) by the Holy Spirit

Did you ask God to fill you with the Holy Spirit? Do you know that you are now filled with the Holy Spirit? On what authority? (On the trustworthiness of God Himself and His Word: Hebrews 11:6; Romans 14:22,23.)

Do not depend upon feelings. The promise of God's Word, not our feelings, is our authority. The Christian lives by faith (trust) in the trustworthiness of God Himself and His Word.

This train diagram illustrates the relationship between **fact** (God and His Word), **faith** (our trust in God and His Word), and **feeling** (the result of our faith and obedience) (John 14:21).

The train will run with or without the caboose. However, it would be futile to attempt to pull the train by the caboose. In the same way, we, as Christians, do not depend upon feelings or emotions, but we place our faith (trust) in the trustworthiness of God and the promises of His Word.

How to Walk in the Spirit

Faith (trust in God and in His promises) is the only means by which a Christian can live the Spirit-directed life. As you continue to trust Christ moment by moment:

A. Your life will demonstrate more and more of the fruit of the Spirit (Galatians 5:22,23) and will be more and more conformed to the image of Christ (Romans 12:2; 2 Corinthians 3:18).

B. Your prayer life and study of God's Word will become more meaningful.

C. You will experience His power in witnessing (Acts 1:8).

D. You will be prepared for spiritual conflict against the world (1 John 2:15-17); against the flesh (Galatians 5:16,17); and against Satan (1 Peter 5:7-9; Ephesians 6:10-13).

E. You will experience His power to resist temptation and sin (1 Corinthians 10:13; Philippians 4:13; Ephesians 1:19-23; 6:10; 2 Timothy 1:7; Romans 6:1-16).

Spiritual Breathing

By faith you can continue to experience God's love and forgiveness.

If you become aware of an area of your life (an attitude or an action) that is displeasing to the Lord, even though you are walking with Him and sincerely desiring to serve Him, simply thank God that He has forgiven your sins — past, present and future — on the basis of Christ's death on the cross. Claim His love and forgiveness by faith and continue to have fellowship with Him.

If you retake the throne of your life through sin — a definite act of disobedience — breathe spiritually.

Spiritual Breathing (exhaling the impure and inhaling the pure) is an exercise in faith and enables you to continue to experience God's love and forgiveness.

1. **Exhale** — confess your sin — agree with God concerning your sin and thank Him for His forgiveness of it, according to 1 John 1:9 and Hebrews 10:1-25. Confession involves repentance — a change in attitude and action.

2. **Inhale** — surrender the control of your life to Christ, and appropriate (receive) the fullness of the Holy Spirit by faith. Trust that He now directs and empowers you, according to the **command** of Ephesians 5:18 and the **promise** of 1 John 5:14,15.

* * * * *

Notes

Chapter One

1. Louis O. Caldwell, *When Partners Become Parents* (Grand Rapids, MI: Baker Book House, n.d.).
2. As quoted in *Why Wait?* by Josh McDowell and Dick Day (San Bernardino, CA: Here's Life Publishers, 1987), p. 60.
3. Armand Nicholi, Jr., "Changes in the American Family," *White House Paper* (October 25, 1984), pp. 7-8.

Chapter Two

1. Dan Benson, *The Total Man* (Wheaton, IL: Tyndale House Publishers, 1977), p. 183.

Chapter Three

1. As quoted in *Why Wait?* by Josh McDowell and Dick Day (San Bernardino, CA: Here's Life Publishers, 1987), p. 33.
2. Kevin Perrotta, "American Youth: A Troubled Generation," *Pastoral Renewal* (November 1983), p. 40.
3. Vance Packard, *Our Endangered Children* (Boston: Little, Brown and Company, 1983), p. xvii.
4. Packard, *Endangered Children,* p. xvii.
5. Perrotta, "American Youth," p. 41.
6. Rodney Clapp, "Vanishing Childhood," *Christianity Today* (May 18, 1984), p. 14.
7. Alan Kenney, "Teens and Sex," *The Arizona Republic* (March 27, 1988), p. C3.
8. As quoted in "TV: Where the Girls Are Good Looking and the Good Guys Win," *Christianity Today* (October 4, 1985), p. 36.
9. Jacqueline Kasun, "Turning Your Children Into Sex Experts," *The Public Interest* (Spring 1979), pp. 3-14.
10. As quoted in "Our Secular Society," *World Wide Challenge* (August 1987), p. 66.
11. *The 108th Edition of Statistical Abstract of the United States* (U.S. Department of Commerce Bureau of the Census, 1988).
12. Alexander Astin, Kenneth Green and William Korn, *The American Freshman: Twenty Year Trends* (Los Angeles: American Council on Education, 1985), p. 22.
13. Kevin Perrotta, "The Better Things Get, The Worse Our Young People Are Doing," *Pastoral Renewal* (May 1987), p. 8.

Chapter Four

1. As quoted in *Evidence That Demands a Verdict,* Vol. 1, by Josh McDowell (San Bernardino, CA: Here's Life Publishers, 1979), p. 366.
2. William Barclay, *The Gospel of John,* Vol. 1 (Philadelphia: Westminster Press, 1975), p. 74.

3. Walter Trobisch, *I Married You* (New York: Harper and Row, 1971), p. 17.

Chapter Five

1. Christopher P. Anderson, *Father: The Figure and the Force* (New York: Warner Books, 1983), pp. 86-87.

2. As quoted in *Why Wait?* by Josh McDowell and Dick Day (San Bernardino, CA: Here's Life Publishers, 1987), pp. 44-45.

3. McDowell and Day, *Why Wait?*, p. 45.

4. McDowell and Day, *Why Wait?*, p. 45.

5. McDowell and Day, *Why Wait?*, p. 45.

Chapter Six

1. Walter Trobisch, *My Beautiful Feelings* (Downers Grove, IL: InterVarsity Press, 1976), p. 22.

2. Trobisch, *Beautiful Feelings*, p. 23.

3. As quoted in *What They Did Right*, Virginia Hearn, ed. (Wheaton, IL: Tyndale House Publishers, 1974), p. 146.

Chapter 7

1. William Stokes, "Intelligent Preparation of Children for Adolescence," *Journal of Marriage and the Family* (May 1965), p. 163.

Chapter Eight

1. Harold Smith, "Superkids and Superparents," *Christianity Today* (September 18, 1987), p. 14.

2. As quoted in *What They Did Right*, Virginia Hearn, ed. (Wheaton, IL: Tyndale House Publishers, 1974), pp. 166-167.

3. Dan Benson, *The Total Man* (Wheaton, IL: Tyndale House Publishers, 1977), p. 181-182.

Chapter Nine

1. Paul D. Meier, *Christian Child-Rearing and Personality Development* (Grand Rapids, MI: Baker Book House, 1977), p. 26.

2. Armand Nicholi, Jr., "Changes in the American Family," *White House Paper* (October 25, 1984), p. 2.

Chapter Ten

1. As quoted in *What They Did Right*, Virginia Hearn, ed. (Wheaton, IL: Tyndale House Publishers, 1974), p. 274.

2. Dennis Rainey, *Pulling Weeds, Planting Seeds* (San Bernardino, CA: Here's Life Publishers, 1989), pp. 29-30.

Chapter Eleven

1. Gordon MacDonald, *The Effective Father* (Wheaton, IL: Tyndale House Publishers, 1977), p. 39.

JOSH MCDOWELL, a traveling representative of Campus Crusade for Christ, a magna cum laude graduate of Talbot Theological Seminary and a member of two national honor societies, is the author of numerous books, including the number-one bestseller, *Why Wait? What You Need to Know About the Teen Sexuality Crisis.* Others are *Teens Speak Out: What I Wish My Parents Knew About My Sexuality; Evidence That Demands a Verdict, Volumes 1 & 2; The Resurrection Factor;* and *The Secret of Loving.* He co-authored his most recent defense of the Christian faith, *He Walked Among Us: Evidence for the Historical Jesus,* with writer-researcher Bill Wilson. Josh and his wife, Dottie, have four children.

DR. NORM WAKEFIELD is a graduate of Moody Bible Institute, Westmont College, and Wheaton College, and holds an Ed.D. from Southern Baptist Theological Seminary. He has authored four books: *Solving Problems Before They Become Conflicts; Listening: The Christian's Guide to Loving Relationships; You Can Have a Happier Family;* and *Building Self-Esteem in the Family.* He is a lecturer and a counselor in the areas of Christian living, family life and leadership development. Dr. Wakefield and his wife, Winnie, have five children.

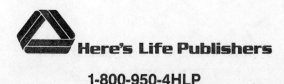